BEGINNER'S GUIDE TO AMAZON KDP: 2023 EDITION

How To Make Money Self-Publishing Fiction, Non-Fiction & Low-Content Books

By Ann Eckhart

TABLE OF CONTENTS

INTRODUCTION

I wrote my first Kindle eBook in December of 2013. After nine years spent selling online (first with new gift items on both Amazon and Ebay and then with secondhand items just on Ebay), I felt burned out spending all my time as a reseller. Sourcing items, taking and editing photographs, writing listings, answering customer questions, and processing orders took a toll on me. I was exhausted and, quite frankly, bored.

In addition, the unsteady income was leaving me stressed and anxious. While holiday sales were terrific, summer sales were dismal as kids were out of school and families went on vacations. June, July, and August were prime sourcing months as people held garage sales, but it was hard to find money to spend when sales were low.

Because I needed to work from home to care for my elderly father, I had to figure out another home-based business to supplement Ebay, not just for the extra money but also to save my sanity. I had a YouTube channel that brought in a little bit of extra money, but not nearly enough to replace what I made on Ebay.

As a child, I had always excelled at writing. It was the one constant in my life, something that every teacher I ever had praised me for. But while my educational studies (from elementary school all the way through college) were focused on English and journalism, I could never figure out how to utilize my writing skills best.

I did not have the "nose for news" a good reporter needs, so newspaper journalism was out. I thought about pursuing magazine writing, but being in Iowa made that difficult as most publications are based in New York. And I did not see myself writing fiction, believing I was only capable of non-fiction.

Eventually, I convinced myself that writing was not a "real" career and sought out other jobs, eventually landing an office position at a local non-profit. After seven years there, I could no longer handle working for someone else and dove into the world of self-employment, which led me to reselling.

However, with reselling wearing me down, I decided to try my hand at writing a book. I honestly do not remember when I realized that you could make money by self-publishing Kindle eBooks on Amazon. I think I might have seen an ad on Amazon when I was ordering Kindle eBooks to read myself. But regardless of how I discovered self-publishing on Amazon, I quickly dove into learning all I could about it.

The more I learned about **Kindle Direct Publishing**, or **KDP** for short, the more I wondered if I, too, could write a book. Could this be a way for me to utilize my writing skills and make money? I remember thinking that if I could write a book that earned me an extra $50 per month, I would consider that a success. An extra $50 a month would pay for my car insurance, which at that time seemed like a great goal.

I started researching the Kindle eBooks available on Amazon and was amazed to find that many of them were self-published by the authors themselves, not through traditional publishing houses. I found that tens of thousands of people were making money – some part-time but others full-time – by self-publishing everything from cookbooks to romance novels.

Certainly, if these folks could publish their books on Amazon, then so could I.

Well, *could* I?

And, more importantly, *how* would I?

Honestly, the HOW of self-publishing an eBook held me back for quite a while. I had no idea how to format and upload a Kindle book. Did I need special word processing software? Would I have to hire someone to format my book for me? How would I design a book cover?

Not knowing where to begin left me stalled. So many other people seemed to be effortlessly self-publishing their books. But how was I supposed to do it? The "how" stopped me from evening trying for months.

Finally, even though I was confused and overwhelmed, I sat down at my computer and started researching how to self-publish a Kindle eBook. And while there were other websites available to self-publish books on, since I was already an experienced Amazon shopper, seller, and Kindle user, I was naturally drawn to learning about self-publishing through Amazon's Kindle Direct Publishing program called Amazon KDP. I read blogs. I skimmed discussion forums. I watched YouTube videos. I overloaded myself with so much information that my head nearly exploded.

It was all too much, and I almost gave up before I even wrote one word. However, I took a deep breath, jotted down the basics, and eventually realized that the KDP self-publishing process was EASY! So many forums and videos made it out to be ridiculously complicated. But I finally sorted through all of the noise and got down to the actual steps, realizing that I could EASILY self-publish a Kindle eBook through Amazon.

And so, I sat down to write my first book. Using my own personal knowledge base, the book was about Ebay. Therefore, most of the book was already written in my brain; I just needed to put it all down on paper. Or, in my case, type it up in Microsoft Word.

Once I wrote and published my first Kindle eBook (which, in the years since, I've completely overhauled and republished), I then set out to promote it. Again, at first, I was overwhelmed by the responsibility of handling my book's marketing on my own. After all, the big-name authors have agents and publishing houses to take care of this back-end work.

However, I soon figured out how to drive sales to my book not only easily and quickly but, for the most part, for FREE using social media. I had a decent following on YouTube, and my subscribers were the ones who initially purchased my books. And I continued adding more books to my library, eventually creating not only a library of books for sale but also a brand.

The first books I wrote were non-fiction, focusing on teaching people how to make money on Ebay and YouTube, plus some short booklets about making money online and saving money when shopping. I even published three travel guides for Walt Disney World. However, for several years, my books were all non-fiction, relatively short, and only available on Kindle.

As the Kindle eBook market became more competitive, I found that my sales were starting to slip. What I had built up to be a full-time income was being pushed back to a part-time level, causing me to have to rely on Ebay again. Making money from eBooks had been a bit of a secret. But once word got out, Amazon became flooded with all types of Kindle books. The market became very crowded, and most authors saw their sales dip.

Desperate to save my publishing business, I knew that I needed to make some changes. And that is when I decided to offer several of my books in paperback on Amazon. Again, just like I had been overwhelmed when I published my first Kindle eBook, I was anxious about releasing paperbacks. The formatting process was different from Kindle; not just the interior but also the covers. Paperback was an option for a couple of years before I finally released my own. Again, my hesitancy cost me tens of thousands of dollars in revenue.

However, just as I had eventually taught myself to self-publish Kindle books, I found that Amazon made publishing paperback books just as easy. And once again, I kicked myself for waiting so long. My royalties doubled the first month my books were available in paperback form. And one year after that, my royalties doubled again when I released new updated versions of my books.

Once I published my first paperback book, formatting and uploading the others was second nature. I improved on the books overall, expanding them so that they offered more value to readers but also so that I could charge more for them. I had initially priced my Kindle eBooks at $3.99 each. But by making them longer, I could increase the price to $9.99. And I could charge upwards of $16.99 for each of my paperback books.

When I finally had paperback versions of my books available, I found that most customers preferred paperbacks to eBooks. My sales skyrocketed, and today my paperback book sales outsell my Kindle eBooks ten to one, providing me a full-time level income. I no longer have to sell on Ebay to pay my bills (although I still do here and there because I like the extra money!).

For a couple of years, I was content with just my non-fiction books. After all, they sold well for me. But then my eyes were opened to the possibilities that existed with two other types of books: low-content books and fiction books.

I first discovered low-content books in 2019 when a successful author friend offered a course. She had been creating notebooks, journals, and planners and selling them on Amazon. These no-and-low content books (referring to the fact that they have little to no writing) had become a popular offering on Amazon and were another way to make money.

I took her course and started a second pen name to upload novelty notebooks, guided journals, and planners with fun cover designs. Eventually, I also added adult coloring books to the collection. And in 2022, I even started an Etsy sticker shop under the same brand name.

No-and-low content books have added a consistent extra $1,000 a month to my income, and during the fourth quarter, that number quadruples as people buy these products as gifts. While they don't bring in the same amount of sales and profit that my non-fiction books do, creating these products is easy and fun, and they give me a break from my more tedious work.

Once I mastered no-and-low content books, I decided to try my hand at writing fiction. The same author friend who had offered a course on low-content books had already created a course for fiction books. She had built her business up to making six figures a month (you read that right: over $100,000 every MONTH!), so I knew I could trust her advice.

As I mentioned, I had not believed myself to be a fiction writer, convinced that writing non-fiction was my only skill. Other than a creative writing course in high school, I had honestly never given fiction much thought. But, when I saw how much my author friend and her counterparts were making self-publishing fiction books (which was a lot more than non-fiction book publishers were making), I decided to explore the possibility for myself.

So, in the summer of 2020, I took the leap into writing my first fiction book. In my friend's course, I learned not only about how to write fiction books but also how to market them. I also browsed Facebook author groups and watched YouTube videos for advice, soaking in all the information that I could. Finally, however, I just dove in head first, releasing my first fiction book in July, followed by three more books by the end of the year. The following year I started a second pen name for another genre of fiction.

Today I publish non-fiction books under my own name, my low-content books under a pen name, and fiction books under two different pen names. Yes, I currently have FOUR pen names! While I update my non-fiction books on a yearly basis, once a fiction book is done, I never have to touch it again. The same is true with my no-and-low content books. However, my low-content and fiction books continually provide me with passive income. And I am continually adding new books to Amazon to sell, increasing my library of titles. It is work I can do from home on my own time schedule and without constantly spending money on inventory to sell on Ebay.

Publishing books to Amazon is by far one of the best ways to make money online from anywhere. All you need is a computer and an internet connection to get started. And while financial success right out of the gate is not likely, if you keep adding books to Amazon, you will begin to see your royalties add up.

In this book, I will walk you step-by-step through the entire Amazon KDP process. From the differences between non-fiction and fiction plus to how to write, edit, upload, and market your books for both Kindle and paperback, this book covers everything from someone who is doing the work and making a living at it. Plus, I will go over how to create no-and-low content books such as journals, planners, and notebooks.

All the information I am about to share with you falls into three different categories:

- **Self-publishing non-fiction Kindle eBooks and paperback books on Amazon**
- **Self-publishing fiction Kindle eBooks and paperback books on Amazon**
- **Self-publishing no-and-low content journals, planners, and notebooks on Amazon**

Note that Amazon does provide other publishing options, including a new hardcover option, audio books, and digital files.

However, in this book, I will be sticking to Kindle eBooks, and paperback books as those are the bulk of the uploads on the site and what everyone starts out with. No-and-low content books cannot be made into eBooks.

Everything I am sharing with you in this book is work I have already done and am currently doing to make Amazon KDP my full-time job. And while overnight success cannot be guaranteed, if you implement the techniques in this book, you, too, will be on your way to making money with self-publishing.

Whether you want to pursue self-publishing non-fiction books, fiction books, no-and-low content books, or a bit of all three the way I do, this book will walk you through all of the steps you need to follow to make your publishing dreams a reality. From writing and editing to formatting and uploading, I will teach you step-by-step the entire self-publishing process.

Not only that, but I will also teach you how to market and advertise your books, including how to run both Facebook and Amazon ads. I've created four unique brands for each of my pen names, and I will teach you how you can do the same.

So, if you are ready to jump into the world of self-publishing, let's get started!

CHAPTER ONE: THE BASICS OF SELF-PUBLISHING

Self-publishing allows writers to skip the traditional route of getting their books into the hands of readers. Rather than sending your manuscript out to agents and publishing houses, hoping and praying for a book deal, you can just upload your work onto a book distribution site. There are no rejection letters, no editors, and no expectations. You write it, you upload it, and the website sells it for you, giving you the profits directly.

The stigma of self-publishing is also diminishing, although I still get comments from people who want to write a "real book" that is mass distributed by a publishing house, however, once they hear about the money self-published authors make versus those who sign over the rights to their work to publishers, their tune changes.

On Amazon, for instance, you can earn up to 70% of the sale price of a Kindle eBook. For paperback books, you earn 60%. If you were traditionally published, you might only make 10%. While I love to write what I want when I want, self-publishing also gives me the freedom to maximize the profits I earn. I do not have to give a cut of the royalties to anyone other than the website I use to publish. At most, the cut is 45% depending on the website and format I publish my books on, much better than handing 90% of the profits over to a publishing house. Oh, and then there is the cut you have to pay your agent.

If you want to make the most money from your books as possible, self-publishing is the way to go. I know of authors who earn six figures a month with their books. That's over one million dollars a year! And while some big-name authors make a lot of money, the vast majority of traditionally published authors barely earn minimum wage after all is said and done.

Self-publishing also allows you total freedom to write what you want and how you want to. You can write short stories or epic novels. You can explore any genre you like: romance, thriller, mystery, children's literature, young adult fiction, or any topic in non-fiction. Love graphic design? Then creating no-and-low content journals, planners, notebooks, and activity books would be right up your alley.

When you self-publish, you do not have to adhere to publisher deadlines. You do not have an editor giving you endless corrections that you do not really want to make. And you do not have to see your royalties eaten up by others when you do all the work. You are in control, and the bulk of the money is yours. My expenses are minimal: some graphic design software and some advertising. After I pay taxes, my profits are mine!

However, that is not to say that the responsibility of doing everything yourself cannot be overwhelming. In addition to writing, you will also need to edit your own work. The cover is your responsibility, and you must format and upload your book yourself. Plus, you then, of course, must promote your book to sell it. No one will do these things for you unless you pay them to do it (hiring an editor, for example). And even when you may hire out some self-publishing tasks, freelance help is much cheaper than the cut publishing houses take at the end of the day. Whatever you decide to do, the final decisions come down to you.

Being your own writer, editor, cover designer, publisher, and advertising agency can seem like an impossible task at first. However, I am here to tell you that it is also incredibly empowering and freeing. You do not have anyone telling you what you should write or how you should write it. You get to be your own one-person self-publishing house with total control over your books.

So why self-publish books specifically on Amazon? After all, there are other self-publishing platforms out there. Simply put, Amazon holds the lion's share of the book market, with nearly 50% of the print book market and 75% of the eBook market. The rest is shared between traditional publishing houses along with Apple Books, Barnes & Noble, Kobo, and Google. Amazon started out as an online bookstore, and they remain the leader in the book category today. And allowing writers to self-publish on their site has only grown their dominance.

Having your book available for Amazon customers to purchase means you will have the vast majority of shoppers worldwide able to purchase your book. I sell my books to customers in the United States, Canada, the U.K., Australia, Japan, Germany, and Italy, but I only have to publish on Amazon.com, which is Amazon's American platform. Amazon does the work of getting my books seen by international buyers. They also handle the printing, shipping, and customer service for the books I sell. My only job is to upload my work.

If my books were traditionally published, I'd first need to hire an agent to get them into the hands of publishers. I'd also need to hire a lawyer who understands the publishing world. My books would likely only be available in America, and I would lose out on hundreds of dollars every month from international sales. If my books proved extremely popular, a publishing house might consider expanding their sales internationally, but there is no guarantee.

And if the book does not do well by a publisher's standards, they would stop printing and promoting it. And they would likely drop me as a client. I have met far too many authors who sold the rights to their books to publishing houses only to have their book be dropped due to sales not meeting a particular threshold. When you self-publish, your book stays on the Amazon website unless you unpublish it. And you can continue to promote it for as long as you would like. You can also expand on your first book by writing more in the same series. The possibilities are endless.

Amazon also offers the best way for authors to make money from their Kindle eBooks, specifically their fiction books, through their **Kindle Unlimited** program, which pays authors when someone borrows one of their eBooks. This means you can make money from both the sale and borrowing of your Kindle titles. We will discuss the Kindle Unlimited program in-depth later in this book.

When you sign up for a KDP account, you can not only upload your book for sale on Amazon, but you can go in at any time and upload a new version of it. Your writing is not set in stone; if you find mistakes or want to include new information, you simply upload a new version onto Amazon, which will replace the old one. Once your book is traditionally published, that is it, as you have signed your rights away.

You can also change your book's price at any time on Amazon. You might initially try pricing a Kindle eBook at $5.99, but you can lower that price if it is not selling. If you have ever bought Kindle eBooks, you know that prices start at 99 cents and go up into the double digits. Your royalty percentage varies based on the price you set. You can adjust your book's price according to market demand, raising the price during peak sales periods and lowering it if sales slow down. And if you choose to be exclusive on Amazon and enroll your book in their Kindle Unlimited program, you can run free promotions and discounts to bring in traffic.

Amazon offers you millions of customers and a super-easy publishing platform with lots of ways for you to promote your work. The question really isn't why would you self-publish on Amazon, but why wouldn't you?

Getting Started: So, you have a book you want to write in mind, and you know you want to publish it through Amazon KDP. Here is the equipment you will need:

Computer: A computer with word processing capabilities. After all, you cannot upload your book to Amazon from a paper notebook or typewriter. And you cannot upload through a smartphone or tablet. So, a computer is necessary, and either a Mac or a PC will do.

Internet: You will need internet access to upload your book to Amazon. The faster the connection, the better.

Microsoft Word: Amazon makes it easy to write and upload books using Microsoft Word software. No fancy writing program is needed, just the standard Microsoft Word that comes with most computer systems. If Word does not come with your system, you can purchase a copy to download online at Microsoft.com or any office supply or big box store.

Graphic Design Software: If you plan to design your own covers, you will need graphics design software and at least one subscription to a commercial graphics site. Note that most writers hire cover designers through websites such as Fiverr and UpWork; making your own is typically reserved for POD products such as planners, journals, and notebooks. But depending on what you are publishing, Amazon also offers a cover designer within KDP that you may find helpful.

And that is it!

Now, I know what you may be thinking: That cannot possibly

be it! Just a computer, internet, and Microsoft Word are all that is standing between me and publishing my book on Amazon? But it is the truth. And while I will be going more in-depth later in this book regarding more sophisticated software and design options, you can absolutely get started with what you likely already have on hand.

As with any business, it is always best to start with what you already have and to upgrade later if you feel you need to. I purchased my current laptop over five years ago and have written numerous books on it. I use the standard internet connection that my cable company provides. And my computer came pre-loaded with Microsoft Word. I have invested in some software for creating book covers, but I also hire some covers out to graphic designers. Self-publishing is genuinely one of the few businesses you can do entirely at home on your computer with little to no investment!

CHAPTER TWO:
THE IMPORTANCE
OF AMAZON BOOK
CATEGORIES

A s I stated in the Introduction of this book, the types of books I will teach you about are fiction, non-fiction, and low-content (journals, planners, notebooks, and activity books). And while some information applies to only one of these types of books, many of the chapters in this book have elements that apply to all three.

This is one of those chapters, as the categories you list your books in greatly impact customers' ability to find them.

Regarding fiction and non-fiction books, Kindle and paperback go hand in hand. Almost all books are first uploaded as Kindle files, and then a paperback version is added to that same listing. If you have shopped for books on Amazon, you have likely noticed that both Kindle and paperback versions are available for many books; you just click on the format you want to purchase.

Note that no-and-low content books are only available in

paperback. However, categories are still important for journals, planners, notebooks, and activity books.

However, before you can upload a book to Amazon, you must either write it (fiction or non-fiction) or design it (low-content). But before you even start to write a book, you need to know the type of book it will be, along with the category it will sell in. That is why I am putting this chapter *before* information about how to format and upload a book, as you cannot self-publish a book on Amazon until you have an actual book. So, we need to tackle that first.

When it comes to the types of books you can write, you are looking at two categories: **fiction** and **non-fiction**. Some publishers, such as myself, do both, while others stick to one. There is no right or wrong choice, and you just need to start with whichever works for you, again understanding that when you self-publish, you can write in any category as your journey continues.

Fiction: I am sure you are already familiar with fiction, which the dictionary defines as "literature in the form of prose, especially short stories and novels, that describes imaginary events and people."

And while you have likely heard of big-name authors, from William Shakespeare and Agatha Christie to Danielle Steel and J.K. Rowling, there are hundreds of thousands of writers who self-publish their fiction books, and most self-publish them on Amazon.

With Amazon paying nearly three times as much as traditional publishers, it is easy to see why authors who have not been able to secure a traditional book deal have turned to Amazon. After all, why go through sending out stacks of proposals and dealing with rejection when you can just sell your book yourself?

Amazon devotes an entire section to *Fiction & Literature* books, and all are available for publishing as both Kindle and paperback. While some authors publish their books in both forms, many start with just Kindle eBooks. The main categories of Kindle eBook fiction on Amazon area:

- Absurdist
- Action & Adventure
- Adaptations & Pastiche
- Animals
- Anthologies & Literature Collections
- Black & African American
- British
- Classics
- Contemporary Fiction
- Drama & Plays
- Erotica
- Essays & Correspondence
- Foreign Language Fiction
- Genre Fiction
- Historical Fiction
- Horror
- Humor & Satire
- Literary Fiction
- Mythology & Folk Tales
- Poetry
- Religious & Inspirational
- Short Stories
- Small Town & Rural
- United States
- Women's Fiction
- World Literature

I am guessing you looked at that list and quickly narrowed down the genre under which the types of fiction books you like to read are under. And you may even look at that list and see the genre in which you want to write. Or you may not see the category of books you read.

Take another look: Do you see *Romance* listed? *Romance* is the largest category of fiction books, yet Amazon does not list it under the main Kindle categories.

Suppose, like with *Romance,* you do not see the Kindle category that your books fall under. In that case, there are two reasons: One, the genre has its own category under Kindle, not under Fiction & Literature (Ah! There you are, *Romance!*); or two, it is under one of the numerous sub-categories.

Let's back up a moment and go back to the main Kindle categories. Click on Kindle Books in the top bar of any Amazon page. You will then see Categories right under it. Clicking on Categories brings up a drop-down menu with the following options:

- Arts & Photography
- Biographies & Memoirs
- Business & Money
- Children's eBooks
- Comics, Manga & Graphic Novels
- Computers & Teaching
- Cookbooks, Food & Wine
- Crafts, Hobbies & Home
- Education & Teaching
- Engineering & Transportation
- Foreign Languages
- Health, Fitness & Dieting
- History
- Humor & Entertainment
- Law
- LGBTQ+ eBooks
- Literature & Fiction
- Medical eBooks
- Mystery, Thriller & Suspense
- Nonfiction
- Parenting & Relationships

- Politics & Social Sciences
- Reference
- Religion & Spirituality
- Romance
- Science Fiction & Fantasy
- Science & Math
- Sports & Outdoors
- Teen & Young Adult
- Travel

As you can see, *Romance* isn't the only genre listed here that one would classify as fiction. And while *Romance* may not be listed directly under the main *Fiction & Literature* category, it does appear as a sub-category in other sections. In fact, there are nearly 80 sub-categories of *Romance* under Kindle eBooks alone!

Like a good fiction book, there is a plot twist when it comes to book categories on Amazon. And you need to understand this twist to find where your books will fall. Remember: Having your books in the correct categories is critical for potential readers being able to find them.

The categories listed above are just the **main** categories of Kindle eBooks. And each of the main categories has numerous **sub-categories**. The genre for your books may be found under multiple sub-categories.

Take the best-selling novel *Where the Crawdads Sing* as an example. The main Kindle category it appears in is *Contemporary Literary Fiction.* However, you can also find it under *Teen & Young Adult* Romance.

Another plot twist? The paperback categories are different from the Kindle versions. The paperback categories have their own **Fiction & Literature** section with their own categories, which are:

- Ancient & Medieval Literature
- Black & African American

- British & Irish
- Classics
- Contemporary
- Drama & Plays
- Erotica
- Essays & Correspondence
- Genre Fiction
- Historical Fiction
- History & Criticism
- Humor & Satire
- Literacy
- Mythology & Folk Tales
- Poetry
- Short Stories & Anthologies
- United States
- Women's Fiction
- World Literature

But look at that list closely. Are some fiction categories missing? Like, maybe, *Romance*? Well, that is because, just like not all Kindle categories cover all genres, the paperback section does not. Instead, you may find your fiction category under the main categories, not under *Fiction & Literature.* As an example, the following categories all have *Romance* sub-categories:

- Christian Books & Bibles
- Comics & Graphic Novels
- Religion & Spirituality
- Self-Help
- Teen & Young Adult

Let's go back to *Where the Crawdads Sing*. Remember how its number one category for the Kindle version was *Contemporary Literary Fiction*? For the paperback version, its first category is *Mothers & Children Fiction*!

Are you confused yet? Please stick with me; I promise I am going to help you make sense of it.

BEGINNER'S GUIDE TO AMAZON KDP: 2023 EDITION

But hold on, as I am going to take you on a bit of a journey first.

When you upload a Kindle eBook to Amazon, you will need to choose two categories for it to be listed under. Then if you upload the paperback version of that Kindle eBook to Amazon, you need to choose two categories for it to be listed under. Sometimes you can find the same categories and subcategories, but sometimes they differ between the two formats, as demonstrated earlier.

Oh, and those sub-categories? Plot twist number two: Many sub-categories also have sub-categories. And some of those sub-categories have sub-categories. We are talking sub-sub-sub-categories in some cases. How will you find where your books fit with thousands of potential categories? And why does it even matter? Why not just plop your book into the two most relevant categories and get on with your life?

The subcategories matter when it comes to making money on Amazon. If you just want to write for the fun of it and do not care about selling any books, then, sure, pick whatever category you want. But I am guessing by now you have realized the potential of making money by self-publishing, which means you should know your book's category, and potentially several other categories it may fall under before you even write it.

Why? Well, the fiction book market on Amazon is enormous, so readers tend to seek out **sub-genres**, also called **troupes,** of the types of stories they like. This search feature, where Amazon provides so many sub-categories, is how self-published authors can get a leg up on the competition, and that is by **writing to market.**

Writing to market means authors actively seek out these unique troupes to find a loyal audience for their books and make more money than they would if they wrote under a standard troupe.

Let's take the *Romance* genre, the largest book category, on Amazon and off. As we've discussed, *Romance* is found under numerous main Kindle and paperback book categories and sub-categories. In this case, I will click on *Books* at the top of the Amazon homepage. On the left side of the page is the **Department** section, and it is here where you find the main book genres, which I laid out earlier.

I am going to click on *Romance*. Amazon will take me to a new page where there are several sub-genres to choose from:

- Action & Adventure
- Black & African American
- Anthologies
- Billionaires
- Clean & Wholesome
- Contemporary
- Erotica
- Fantasy
- Gothic
- Historical
- Holidays
- Inspirational
- LGBTQ+
- Medical
- Military
- Multicultural
- New Adult & College
- Paranormal
- Regency
- Romantic Comedy
- Romantic Suspense
- Science Fiction
- Sports
- Time Travel
- Vampires
- Werewolves & Shifters
- Western
- Writing

Outlander and *Bridgerton* have made *Historical Romance* a popular genre. But wait! Because under the *Historical Romance* category are more sub-categories:

- 20th Century
- American
- Ancient World
- Medieval
- Regency
- Scottish
- Tudor
- Victorian
- Viking

Then readers can narrow down their search by Romantic Heroes:

- Alpha Males
- BBW
- Bikers
- Cowboys
- Criminals & Outlaws
- Doctors
- Firefighters
- Highlanders
- Pirates
- Royalty & Aristocrats
- Spies
- Vikings
- Wealthy

And then there are the Romantic Themes:

- Amnesia
- Beaches
- International
- Love Triangle
- Medical

- Second Chances
- Secret Baby
- Vacation
- Wedding
- Workplace

There are over 50,000 results under the *Secret Baby* sub-genre. However, if I narrow it down further by choosing *Highlanders*, the number of books available drops to 309. Now, rather than trying to compete with over 50,000 other books, you only have to compete with a few hundred.

And this is how you help readers find you. Not by burying your book under one genre or sub-genre, but by choosing the most niche genre you can find. And there is nothing more niche than a historical romance featuring a Highlander and a secret baby!

By now, I am sure your head is spinning. Categories, genres, troupes...and all have multiple layers of sub-categories. And the choices differ based on the Kindle and paperback lists.

But consider all this data a gift, as it will help you focus on your book's theme before you even start writing it! Instead of sitting down and writing a run-of-the-mill romance novel that will get buried among all the others, you have a road map to success. By focusing on a particular niche, you will be able to attract customers more easily to buy your book.

The same holds true if you create low-and-no content books such as journals, planners, notebooks, and activity books. Let's say you want to publish a blank journal with a collage of cartoon cats on the cover. The logical category to list a notebook under is *Diaries & Journals.* But you could also list your journal under one or more of the several *Cats* categories or sub-categories. In fact, you can add each version of your books (Kindle and paperback) to up to eight total categories and sub-categories, which will give your book a much better chance of being seen by potential buyers.

NOTE: I will go over the step-by-step process of creating your book's listing later in this book. But I want to cover the topic of categories first as it is so important to understand before you start writing.

We'll discuss how to list your books in multiple categories coming up, but first, let's get back to how to research the main category for your book. Maybe you already have a book in mind. How can you find the perfect categories and sub-categories for it when there are so many to choose from? The answer is a bit of good old-fashioned research!

First, look up the books that fit your genre. On the book's Amazon page, you will find what categories the book is in. Let's use *Harry Potter* as an example. If you type *Harry Potter* into the Amazon search bar, it will bring up everything *Harry Potter*-related on the site, not just the books but also the movies and merchandise. However, on the left-hand side of the page, you can narrow down your search under *Department.*

Note that you will see both a **Books** option and a **Kindle Store** option. Remember, the categories vary between the two. For this example, let's click on the *Kindle Store* option. You can then click on *Kindle eBooks*, which will bring up a handful of sub-categories. But for this example, let's just select a book from the main page. I click on *Harry Potter: The Complete Collection,* which takes me directly to the book's information page.

Scrolling down the product page takes me to a section titled **Product details**. Here are all the technical aspects of the book, everything from the ASIN and publication date to the language and print length.

The book's **Best Sellers Rank** is at the end of this block of information. This is where you can see the main categories the book is in. For the Kindle version of this Harry *Potter* set, it lists the following subcategories:

- Teen & Young Adult Humor Nonfiction eBooks

- Fantasy Anthologies & Short Stories
- Children's Coming of Age Fantasy Books

Are you shocked to read those categories? *Humor Nonfiction*? *Short Stories*? For *Harry Potter*? What is going on?

Remember: There are hundreds of categories and subcategories available. Putting your book into a general category will likely result in your book being buried in Amazon's search.

However, putting your book into sub-categories, **even categories that do not match your genre,** can help you increase your overall rank. And on Amazon, rank is everything. With so many books on their website and more being loaded every single day, your book's rank is essential in helping readers find your titles.

Okay, then, but why are three categories listed when I have told you that you can only select two categories when you upload your book? That leads us to a trick that many authors do not know about: While you can only *manually* choose two categories for your book when you upload it, **you can ask Amazon to add your book to up to eight more categories**. Yes, you read that right: Your book can be added to up to ten categories, which will give your book an even better chance of readers finding it.

Again, I will be walking you step-by-step through the listing process in Chapter Six. But it's so important to understand categories before you even start writing.

So, while it is important to ensure your book is in all the most relevant categories, you may have the opportunity to put it into others. But why put it in categories that are not even accurate? That has to do with rank, which we touched on earlier.

Every single category and sub-category on Amazon has its own best-sellers list. Of course, it is nice when your book is ranked high in the category that perfectly fits it. But if you put your book into smaller niche categories, even some that do not match the theme, it has the chance of ending up on that category's best-seller list.

Here is an example: There is a popular guided journal that is the number one best-selling book in the *Juggling* category. Does this journal have anything to do with juggling? No. The circus? Nope. Is it a journal for jugglers? Not in the slightest. This journal has nothing to do with juggling, yet because the *Juggling* sub-category is so small, the publisher of this book has been able to reach the category's number one spot, which gives it best-seller status. This journal is then given *Number One Best-Seller* status by Amazon, which means customers are more likely to purchase it over similar books.

This book not only has the stamp of *Best Seller* next to its title, but it earns nearly $4,000 per month. All because the publisher found a small sub-category to list it under. It is likely that the publisher chose the two best categories for the book when it was first uploaded and then contacted Amazon afterward, asking for it to be added to eight others. Including *Juggling*!

When I upload a book to Amazon, I choose the two most popular categories for it. I then research additional categories that are a good fit for it, and I send Amazon a message asking them to add my title to those categories. And since the categories for Kindle and paperback differ, I must do this for both versions.

How to contact Amazon to add your book to additional categories: I am including this section both here as well as later on in this book since it is so important to the process. Adding your books into multiple categories is key in helping sell books.

Amazon doesn't make contacting them easy. They would prefer to send you to articles on the site that will likely solve your problem. But in the case of wanting to add your book to additional categories, you need to message them directly.

From your **Kindle Direct Publishing** account page, simply click on **Help** at the top of the page. You can also access the Help section from your **Amazon Author Central** page.

You will be taken to a new page with a list of **HELP TOPICS** on the right.

The last line on this list is **Contact Us.**

Click on *Contact Us.* You will be taken to a new page titled **How can we help?**

Select **Amazon Book Page**.

And then select **Update Amazon categories.**

A **contact form** will then appear for you to fill out. You will need to provide the following:

- **Format:** ASIN or ISBN =
- **Marketplace:** The Amazon site your book is for sale on. In America, this would be .com.
- **Book format:** Kindle or paperback
- **Category:** Using this book, *Beginner's Guide To Amazon KDP*, as an example, I would type in *Kindle Store: Kindle eBooks: Business & Money: Industries: E-commerce: Auctions & Small Business* (this is the main category the Kindle version of this book is in)

I would then repeat the *Category* section for the additional categories I want Amazon to manually list my Kindle book.

After clicking **Send message**, I would then create another request form for the paperback version of the book.

The option to add a total of twenty categories and sub-categories for each of my titles gives my books a much better chance of being found by readers and potentially reaching a best-seller list. I once released a book that was number one in a small sub-category for several weeks, meaning it had a Number One New Release badge next. Even now, months later, that book remains in the top ten of that one category. A category it wouldn't have been listed in had I not contacted Amazon directly.

Oh, and those two categories within the book's listing (again, I will walk you through this step later on in this book)? You can change the categories within your book's listing any time you want. And you can contact Amazon to have them manually change them at any time. Since it is nearly impossible to remember every category in which you have asked Amazon to place your book, keeping a spreadsheet or even a notebook with all the categories recorded is a good idea.

Non-Fiction: The dictionary defines "non-fiction" as "prose writing that is based on facts, real events, and real people, such as biography or history." The categories for non-fiction books break down the same way as fiction because there are different categories and sub-categories for both Kindle eBooks and paperback books.

Just as I did for fiction books, let's look at the non-fiction categories for both Kindle and paperback. The difference here is that Amazon offers *Non-Fiction* as a main category under both Kindle and paperback. However, many of their main categories also cover non-fiction. Selecting the main *Non-Fiction* category will bring up several sub-categories, so for this example, we will focus our attention there. Just note that for my non-fiction books, I choose from the main categories and the subcategories.

The *Non-Fiction* subcategories for Kindle eBooks are:

- Arts & Photography
- Biographies & Memoirs
- Business & Investing
- Children's Nonfiction
- Computers & Technology
- Cooking, Food & Wine
- Crafts, Hobbies & Home
- Education & Reference
- Engineering & Transportation
- Health, Fitness & Dieting
- History

- Law
- Literary Criticism & Theory
- Medical eBooks
- Parenting & Relationships
- Politics & Social Sciences
- Science
- Self-Help
- Sports Travel

Now, just like with fiction books, there are a lot of sub-categories for non-fiction. For instance, most of my non-fiction books fall under the main *Non-Fiction* category and then the *Business & Investing* sub-category. However, under *Business & Investing* are over twenty sub-categories. I typically publish under the *Entrepreneurship & Small Business* sub-category, but even there, I must select from eight sub-categories. And yes, most of those have more sub-categories, too.

Like fiction books, when I upload a non-fiction book to Amazon, I choose two categories for the Kindle version and two for the paperback version. I then contact Amazon and ask them to add each version to eight additional categories I had researched beforehand. I can go into my KDP dashboard anytime and manually change the original two categories. I can contact Amazon anytime and ask them to change additional categories. I keep track of all the categories each of my books is in on a spreadsheet.

All this talk of categories sounds like a lot, I know. But trust me when I tell you that it will make more sense once you are dealing with choosing categories for your own books. It all comes together once you have your finished book ready to publish. And as you publish more and more books, you will see first-hand how the categories you choose affect your book rankings.

Why am I even talking about these categories if they will not matter until you are ready to upload? Well, I want to give you an idea about all the different types of books you can self-publish.

From romance and horror to cookbooks and self-help, in order to self-publish, you just need to find your niche and go from there. You may already have a book in mind, and knowing about categories may help you hone in on a niche trope. Or you may want to make money self-publishing but have no idea what sells. Amazon's categories help for both situations.

But even better than choosing a niche is knowing that you do not have to stick with just one. Most writers who self-publish full-time write all types of books in different genres. The trick is that they write these different books using different pen names. Yes, Amazon and other self-publishing sites allow you to publish under any name you choose, your legal name, or a pen name you develop.

I have four pen names now, and I plan to add more. I write business non-fiction under my own name. I have a print-on-demand pen name for my planners, journals, notebooks, and activity books. And I have two pen names for my fiction books. I am currently considering releasing more fiction books in different genres under new pen names.

Why different pen names for different genres? The answer is simple: **Branding.**

Creating a **brand** is essential for selling books. It is what will keep readers coming back and buying your new releases. I have built a brand under my own legal name around teaching people about being self-employed and making money online. I do not want to dilute my brand by adding non-business-related books under my name, which would confuse my readers.

The non-fiction books I write under my own name are business-related. It would be strange for me also to write thrillers or humor under my own name. Customers would look at my author page and wonder why someone was writing books about Ebay and, say, zombies. It would erode consumer confidence in my books overall.

Note: I do not actually write about zombies. I am just using the genre as an example. However, zombie books are extremely popular!

A lot of what happens with books is that customers latch onto an author and will read all their titles. I often hear from readers who have read all my business books because that is the content they are most interested in. They do not follow me for my fiction books; most do not even know I write fiction under a pen name, and I prefer to keep it that way.

On the flip side, my fiction readers follow me for the type of fiction books I write. They do not follow me for business advice. They do not even know that I sell on Ebay, make YouTube videos, or create journals, planners, and notebooks. To them, I am the author of the fiction books they enjoy reading. My fiction books are a different brand than my non-fiction books.

My planners, journals, notebooks, and activity books are under a different pen name, a pen name with its own brand. In fact, in 2022, I expanded my low-content brand by merging it with an Etsy sticker shop. It's a completely different business than my non-fiction and fiction author brands. My pen names do not overlap, and I run them as though they are separate businesses, even though they are all published under my one Amazon KDP account.

I should note here that I do promote my low-content books and Etsy sticker shop to those who follow me for my non-fiction books. Many have been following my content for years, so I felt comfortable sharing the other "business" I have created with them. However, I do not promote my fiction books on my non-fiction or low-content pages. It's one thing to overlap with my non-fiction and low-content books, but fiction is a whole other genre that wouldn't make sense to combine with my other products.

As I mentioned, I am looking to release new fiction books in other genres; and I will do so using other pen names. Again,

I do not want to confuse or drive away potential readers by lumping different fiction genres under one pen name. Most people know that Steven King writes horror. Well, wouldn't it be strange if he suddenly started publishing historical romance novels? Or releasing gardening tutorials? Several well-known authors publish under multiple pen names. J.K. Rowling wrote *Harry Potter* under her own name but later released the book *The Cuckoo's Calling* under the pen name Robert Galbraith.

A tip about pen names: Many authors use different versions of their legal names to create their pen names, such as using their full first name for one pen name, a nickname for another, and their initials for a third. Other writers use family names, a mix of celebrity names, or just names that they are drawn to.

You may be thinking that managing multiple pen names seems like it would be too difficult. But the fact is that most self-publishers are uploading all types of books under multiple pen names. Amazon and the other self-publishing websites allow multiple pen names under one account and make entering in multiple pen names easy. As we will discuss later in this book, on Amazon, you simply need to enter a name when you upload a book. The only issue you would have is if you tried to use a famous author's name. You cannot upload your books and use Steven King as your pen name.

However, this does not mean that you must write in multiple genres under multiple pen names. You want to start by focusing on publishing one book. Just one! Some authors only have books under one pen name, while others have dozens. Categories and pen names are two things you have total control of when self-publishing.

Perhaps you want to write a historical romance. But after publishing a few novels under that genre, you decide you want to write some cookbooks. No problem! You can simply create another pen name and upload your cookbooks with that pen name.

Whether you ultimately decide to stick with one pen name or expand to multiple ones, the choice is yours. Neither way is right or wrong, and you can change your mind as you go along. I never thought I would write fiction or publish print-on-demand products. But eventually, I decided to try those genres, hence why I currently have three pen names with more on the way. The unlimited choices are the best part of self-publishing.

And now that you have an understanding about how categories are essential to being a successful self-published author, you can focus on actually getting started with Amazon KDP!

CHAPTER THREE: KINDLE, PAPERBACK... OR BOTH

S o, you have your computer with internet access and Microsoft Word. You either already have an idea for a book or have been inspired by looking through Amazon's book categories. It is almost time to get down to writing.

Almost!

While you may already be thinking ahead to the formatting and uploading process you will need to tackle once your book is finished, there is no sense worrying about those things until you have an actual book to publish. And there are still decisions to be made.

Because you will be self-publishing your book, you can write any type of book you would like, whether it is fiction or non-fiction, one page or one thousand pages. Maybe writing isn't what you are interested in; instead, you want to make fun notebooks and planners. YOU are your own publisher and editor, so the decisions are all yours.

Maybe you want to write a book of poems. Go for it! Perhaps you have an idea for a science fiction series. Do it! Maybe you want to design your own adult coloring books. You can do it! Whatever is in your heart and mind to write or create, just do it!

But there is also the small thing about wanting to make MONEY with your books, right? At least, I hope you want to make money because there is money to be made. So, you will need to do more than just write.

There are two different schools of thought when it comes to publishing non-fiction and fiction books for profit on Amazon:

1. Publish many short Kindle eBooks, understanding that you will make most of your money from Kindle Unlimited page reads.
2. Publish fewer but higher quality books that you can sell in Kindle and paperback formats and charge more money.

Both business models work for self-publishing. Some writers choose one, while others do a mix of both. For many years, I did both. I had several short "booklets" available on Kindle and longer books published on Kindle and paperback. I made money on the short books via Kindle Unlimited while making money on the sale of the books not in KDP Select.

Oh, I guess we need to talk about Kindle Select, don't we? Because that adds an entirely new layer to self-publishing on Amazon. But first, a little backstory.

When I first started self-publishing books on Amazon, Kindle was the only option available. Paperback had not been introduced yet. Back then, most Kindle eBooks were short and cheap, typically around $2.99. Amazon also allowed Prime members to download one free Kindle eBook per month, and authors were paid the same amount on those free downloads as they were for their sales.

Initially, I made a lot of money from Prime members choosing my book as their monthly "free" Kindle title. Amazon paid other authors and me out of the Prime membership fees, so I never lost out on money. And I had plenty of other customers who were willing to pay for my books.

In my first month of self-publishing on Amazon, I made $200 with just one book. In four months, I was earning a full-time income from several $2.99 Kindle eBooks. There seemed to be no limit to how high my income would grow as long as I kept consistently publishing short $2.99 Kindle books.

Then along came *Kindle Unlimited,* which drastically changed the self-publishing market on Amazon.

Kindle Unlimited: Kindle Direct Publishing, or KDP for short, is the program you sign up for in order to upload books for sale on Amazon. **KDP Select** is an *optional* program that you can opt into. Enrolling in *KDP Select* means you commit that your book's digital (Kindle eBook) format is available exclusively through Amazon for at least 90 days.

When you enroll a book in *KDP Select,* you cannot publish it on any other website for the time it is enrolled in the program. *This is referred to as being exclusive to Amazon.* You can, however, publish your paperback version elsewhere. There is no *KDP Select* option for paperback books. Customers can "borrow" Kindle books but must "buy" paperback books.

Enrolling your books (and you can choose to enroll only some books, not all, if you would like, as you enroll each book individually) means they will be available to Amazon customers to borrow IF they have a **Kindle Unlimited** subscription. Subscribers can borrow as many eligible Kindle eBooks as they want, and publishers are paid from the subscription fees.

You may think that you do not want anyone to borrow your book; you want them to BUY it. The good part of enrolling your book in *KDP Select* is that Amazon will pay you any time someone borrows and reads your book. Every month, Amazon allocates money from the *Kindle Unlimited* subscription fees into the **KDP Select Global Fund.** The money from this fund is then divided up and given to the authors whose books have been borrowed and read.

The key word here is READ. Customers must now READ the book they download, not just borrow it, for the author to be paid. Let me explain:

Before *Kindle Unlimited*, the average payout to publishers was around $2 per book borrowed. It didn't matter whether or not the customer actually opened and read the file. The simple act of them downloading the book automatically meant the author was paid.

However, in 2015, Amazon made some significant changes to how authors made money on these borrowed books, drastically changing how profits were distributed. No longer were authors going to be paid for downloads; now, they would only be paid when the book file was opened.

In 2015, Amazon launched Kindle Unlimited, an extra-cost subscription service available to *Amazon Prime* members. *Kindle Unlimited* subscribers can *borrow* as many eligible books as they want. I stress *eligible* because most of the books in the *Kindle Select* program, the program writers opt into allowing their books to be available to borrow, are from self-published authors such as myself. The big-name writers with major book deals do not have their books available to be borrowed; Kindle readers only have the option to purchase those titles. So, for the people buying *Kindle Unlimited* memberships, the available titles are primarily from self-published authors.

When I started selling my books via Kindle, I priced them at $2.99 and made $2.07 for every book sold. I also averaged around $2 for any book that was borrowed. Remember, in the beginning, Amazon Prime Members could borrow one free Kindle book per month. When a book sold, we authors were paid whether the customer read the book or not. I was making money on both sales and from those who downloaded my books as part of the Prime subscription.

With the introduction of *Kindle Unlimited*, the readers could now borrow multiple Kindle books, and they only had to make it 10% of the way into the book before the author received payment for the borrowed book. The payout came from the money Amazon made from selling the *Kindle Unlimited* membership. For a small fee, customers could access tens of thousands of books. And self-published authors were making money on both sales and borrows of their books. It was a great set-up, and many self-published authors did well....until the potential money-making opportunity of *Kindle Unlimited* attracted some unsavory types to the site.

Kindle Unlimited soon began what established Kindle authors referred to as the "scam-phlet" craze, i.e., "scam pamphlets." Internet marketers quickly realized that super short books could make money as people only needed to open a book up to the cover to reach Kindle's 10% *KDP Select* threshold for payment. With *Kindle Unlimited*, Prime members, who before were only allowed one free Kindle book borrow per month, could now pay the *Kindle Unlimited* membership fee to get as many eligible books as they wanted. The more books people downloaded and opened up, the more money authors made.

An entire small industry of "Kindle Publishers" (so named as they weren't actual writers) sprang up and played on the strategy of flooding the market with short "books" (no longer than pamphlets in many cases). These publishers knew they only needed people to open the book file up to the 10% mark. And by putting up super short books, just opening the Kindle file to the front page often reached the 10% threshold.

These marketers sought out niche sub-categories to stand out from the crowd. For instance, cookbooks sell well on Kindle, so they looked for a particular type of cooking technique with only a few or even no titles. Once an underserved sub-category was discovered, these marketers would outsource the book writing using freelancing services. For anywhere from $50 to $250, they would find someone to throw together a short booklet for them, one that met the 10% reading mark when only opened to the cover. The book did not have to be any good; it just needed a catchy enough title and cover art to encourage a customer to download it and open it up. It was easy to put up a 10-page recipe booklet for a super-specific ingredient, for example. The marketers didn't care about the quality of the product; they only cared about getting customers to download and open the file.

And because *Kindle Unlimited* subscribers felt that they were getting "free" books, even though they were paying a monthly fee, downloads across Amazon skyrocketed. Since the eligible books were limited, *Kindle Unlimited* subscribers were willing to download almost anything. And marketers fed their desire for books by constantly uploading new content, sometimes hundreds of books a month.

After these junk books went live on Amazon, many "hacks" were used to quickly move copies and generate reviews. Tactics to get the book downloaded included giving away free copies and paying for people to leave reviews. Keyword spamming was also used. While these scammers were touting that they were making six figures on Kindle, what they never disclosed were the thousands of dollars they were paying to produce and sell the books and get them reviewed. However, in another move to make money, they developed paid courses to teach others the same techniques, resulting in thousands of "publishers" jumping on the Kindle bandwagon.

Soon the Kindle market was flooded with so much junk that legitimate books were pushed down to the bottom of searches. The "scam-phlets," with their spammed keywords and fake reviews, rose to the top of the reader lists, which resulted in more downloads.

However, once actual *Kindle Unlimited* customers downloaded these junk books, the negative reviews would start piling up. But the scammers just forged ahead, creating new short reads that would make them money simply by being opened. Because you can have unlimited pen names on Amazon, it took a new niche to target under a new pen name to stay in the game. It was a never-ending cycle of junk books flooding the market, and real authors saw their sales numbers go down every month. In a matter of months, I went from earning a full-time income to barely making enough to pay my car payment.

It did not take long for Amazon to catch on to this "scam-phlet" scheme, mainly because *Kindle Unlimited* customers were not just complaining about all the bad books but also started canceling their memberships. Just as Prime memberships are where Amazon makes most of its money, selling *Kindle Unlimited* subscriptions has also proven to be a big money maker for the site. Amazon knew they needed to save the program. And fast.

To keep customers subscribed to *Kindle Unlimited,* Amazon knew they had to discourage junk books; again, most of these short reads were only making money by simply being opened to the cover and meeting the 10% read threshold. To stop this practice, Amazon drastically changed the payout for borrowed books. Instead of paying authors based on a book being read to the 10% mark, now authors would be paid based on the number of PAGES someone read, which for Amazon meant that they made it to the final page in the book. After all, they reasoned, why would anyone jump from the cover to the back of the book?

Well, the scammers knew how to get readers to the last page of a book. A new workaround began happening where a link would be put on the book's first page enticing the reader to click on it; the link would take them to the back page of the book. And Amazon would record the book as being read, paying out the total amount for the borrow. Readers were promised a secret piece of information, a freebie, or some other hook to get them to go from page one to the last page in the book as soon as the book was opened on Kindle.

Legitimate authors joined alongside readers in complaining about the program, and Amazon decided to take a further step of shutting down "scam-phlets" by going after one of the most significant Kindle publishing tactics: paying people to leave book reviews. Positive product reviews are the key to selling items online, and Kindle eBooks are no different. Reviews can make or break a book's sales, and people on sites such as Fiverr.com were selling "gigs" to leave positive book reviews for as little as $5 per review. Amazon saw this and filed suit against over one thousand Fiverr sellers for violating the terms of Amazon's site by leaving paid reviews.

The lawsuits against the Fiverr sellers are what finally knocked a lot of the "Kindle publishers" out. While they themselves were not sued, they knew they were likely next on the list. Many, but not all, of the "scam-phlets" were pulled, and the courses on how to get rich with Kindle disappeared. Still, the damage was done. There were still those out there trying to manipulate the Kindle system, but more than that, the reputation of self-published authors was tarnished.

Amazon finally made the most significant change to the *Kindle Unlimited* program, one that has helped eliminate the junk books but one that has also made making money from *KDP Select* more difficult. Now **Amazon pays authors per page read,** and their software tracks the turning of the pages. Skipping straight to the back of the book no longer works in terms of authors getting paid.

This would be a welcome development if the per-page payout were better. However, the payout amount is currently around half a cent per page. That's right: Authors now earn ONE PENNY for every two pages a customer reads. That's much less than the over $2 we used to make per borrowed book. If someone only skims a few pages, we are lucky to make a couple of pennies. And if a customer downloads a book but never reads it (which is very common for *Kindle Unlimited* subscribers to do), we are not paid at all.

However, it is not all doom and gloom regarding publishing your book on Kindle. Despite the drop in author profits, Kindle remains the leader in eBook self-publishing. While you can publish your eBooks on other sites, if you opt into the *Kindle Select* program, you can only publish your book on Kindle. Again, though, you can decide on each book individually, not for your overall account. You can have one book in *KDP Select* but opt out of the others. And the enrollment minimum is only 90 days.

And there are plenty of customers who still actually purchase books, regardless of if they have a *Kindle Unlimited* membership or not. None of my non-fiction books are in *Kindle Select*, and I get plenty of sales. It really depends on the categories you are publishing in and if you have an established brand. I started in *Kindle Select*, but once I had an audience of repeat customers, I was able to opt out and rely strictly on sales.

However, I do enroll my fiction books in *Kindle Select*. Since fiction is a new endeavor for me, enrolling my fiction books in *Kindle Select* is the best way to get people to download my books. It's more about getting my books read and gaining a following versus making money. *Kindle Select* is a great way to launch a pen name with the hope that, eventually, your following will grow enough that you can pull your books from the program and only have them available to buy.

Since Amazon still gets the lion's share of eBook readers, my advice would be to opt your books into *Kindle Select* for 90 days, which is the minimum time frame to commit to. See how your book performs; if you are getting frequent borrows that result in many pages being read, you will likely make more money off those borrows (even at only one penny per two pages) than you would be publishing your book to lesser used sites. But if after an initial 90-day trial you are not happy, you can always opt out of *Kindle Select* and add your book to other sites. Or, if you only want to remain on Kindle, you can still opt out, meaning your book is only on Amazon and only available for purchase, not borrow.

And as we've already discussed, the paperback versions of your books can only be offered for sale. There is no *Kindle Select* program for paperbacks. Non-fiction books, in my experience, sell better in paperback, while fiction readers prefer the Kindle format. Fiction customers are often ferocious readers who read book after book, which is great for fiction authors as the demand for their work never seems to end.

I know some authors who remain exclusive to Amazon even though their books are not enrolled in *Kindle Select.* Even after I pulled my books from the *Kindle Select* program, it still took me a couple of years to upload them to **Draft2Digital** for distribution to Apple, Barnes & Noble, and other websites. I will talk more about Draft2Digital later in this book.

If you do choose to enroll in *Kindle Select,* however, there are some marketing tools you can use, such as running promotions. Amazon offers two promotional tools: **Kindle Countdown Deals** and **Free Book** offers.

Kindle Countdown allows you to discount your book on a "countdown" clock basis. For instance, if your book is usually priced at $6.99, you could offer it for 99 cents one day, $1.99 the next, $2.99 the following day, and so on until the clock runs out. *Kindle Countdown* deals can be run for a total of five days per 90-day enrollment period.

The **Free Book** promotional tool lets you offer your book for FREE for up to five days. Each book you have on Kindle is eligible for up to five days of a free book promotion once every 90-days. And your book is not just free to *Kindle Unlimited* subscribers; it is free to anyone using Amazon's website.

While you can offer a book for free for up to five days in a row, you do not have to do it for that long. You can break up those days and run the promotion for one day, two days, three days, four days, or the full five in a row. You can also cancel the promotion anytime if you change your mind.

I personally find that free book promotions work best when you offer the book for free for two- or three-day blocks as it gives customers time to find your book. I like to offer a book for a two-day free promotion and then a three-day free promotion a month or so later. If I keep the book enrolled in *Kindle Select*, I will rerun the promotions in the next 90-day cycle.

Paperback Books: Whether you opt into KDP Select, it is assumed that you will self-publish your books, fiction and/or non-fiction, to Kindle. But what about paperback?

At the beginning of this chapter, I mentioned that one business model for self-publishing is to upload a lot of shorter books, specifically non-fiction, to Kindle and make your money from *Kindle Unlimited* page reads. I have warned you about uploading "scam-phlets," those short junk books favored by scammers. But that does not mean shorter, quality Kindle books are not a reliable business model. They are, and many authors make a living with this "quantity and quality" strategy.

However, producing longer books allows you also to offer your book in paperback. And there are some non-fiction categories where books do better in paperback than they do solely on Kindle. Amazon requires all paperback books to have a minimum page count of 24-pages.

When I published solely on Kindle, my average word count was 15,000 words. Today my non-fiction books average 55,000 words, making them great for Kindle and for paperback, with page counts averaging around 125-pages each. However, my books are primarily non-fiction. Readers expect different minimum page counts for different genres, such as

- Flash Fiction: 300 to 1,500 words
- Short Story: 1,500 to 30,000 words
- Novellas: 30,000 to 50,000 words
- Novels: 50,000 to 100,000 words
- Children's Chapter Books: 4000 to 10,000 words
- Children's Picture Books: 300 to 800 words
- Children's Early Readers: 200 to 3,500 words
- Children's Middle Grade: 25,000 to 40,000 words
- Non-Fiction Memoirs: average of 80,000 words
- Non-Fiction Self-Help: average of 40,000 words

As we discussed early on in this book, fiction has many genres and subcategories, also called troupes. Some of these have their own expected word count, including:

- Mainstream Romance: 70,000 to 100,000 words
- Subgenre Romance: 40,000 to 100,000 words
- Science Fiction/Fantasy 90,000 to 150,000 words
- Historical Fiction: 80,000 to 100,000 words
- Thrillers/Horror/Mysteries/Crime: 70,000 to 90,000 words
- Young Adult: 50,000 to 80,000 words

Do you see the genre you would like to write in listed above? If you do and are taken aback by the expected word count, remember that these are guiding points and averages. I have non-fiction books that fall short of the 40,000-word count, and I have fiction books that hover between novellas and novels. The important thing is to have an idea of what readers expect. After all, they are the ones you hope will purchase your book.

And the longer your book is, the more money you can charge for it. It is hard to sell a book for $10 that is only one thousand words unless it is a children's picture book. And if you plan to release your books both on Kindle and in paperback, the page count is something to keep in mind so that you can confidently sell both digital and physical copies.

Having your books available in paperback also allows you to upload them to other websites. If your Kindle eBooks are enrolled in *Kindle Select*, the eBook version of that book must remain exclusive to Amazon. However, the paperback (and hardcover or audio book) does not. You can "go wide" with your paperback by making it available to readers using Apple, Barnes & Noble, and even libraries. I will talk more about "going wide" later in this book. But for right now, just remember that the higher quality and longer page count a book is, the better it will do in paperback.

Journals, notebooks, planners, and activity books are almost all exclusively in paperback. There are some types of puzzle books that people have published on Kindle, but for the most part, no-and-low content books are strictly offered in paperback.

Note that one format I haven't touched on is hardcover. Amazon does allow you to publish your books in hardcover, although the cost is quite high. When you self-publish a book on Amazon, there are fees involved. There is a small fee for Kindle books to cover the digital files that Amazon stores on their servers. And there is a printing fee for paperback and hardcover books. The printing fee for the hardcover books makes them too expensive for me to make a profit on.

For example, I price my top-selling non-fiction books at $9.99 for the Kindle versions and $16.99 for the paperback versions. The prices are different, but I make the same amount in royalties regardless of which version the customer buys. Why? Because of the printing cost of paperback books. The printing cost comes out of the price of the book, and then Amazon takes a cut of the profits, leaving me with my royalties. I have to charge more for my paperback books to make as much as the Kindle versions to account for the printing fees.

But to sell my books in hardcover, I would have to charge $24.99 to make the same amount of money as I do when I sell a Kindle or paperback copy. That cost is simply too high for what the customer receives, especially since Amazon's hardcover books don't have dust jackets. Regarding quality, there is little difference between Amazon's paperback books and their hardcover books. Hence why I rarely publish my books in hardcover.

However, some books do well in hardcover, such as large format books. For example, offering a hardcover version may make sense if you are publishing an 8.5x11-inch book with lots of color photos. Once you know what category you will publish your book in, look at what formats other authors in the genre offer. If none of them have their books available in hardcover, it won't make much sense for you to offer a hardcover version.

Kindle, paperback...or both. Each has an active reader base, and each format can earn you money. I employ the "quality over quantity" method for self-publishing; I do not have hundreds of non-fiction and fiction books published, but the ones I do are good enough to not only be eBooks but also paperbacks. And I also have various sizes of paperback low-content books I've created.

If you plan to write fiction or non-fiction, it's tempting to just publish Kindle versions and not worry about formatting paperback covers. However, you are leaving money on the table by not exploring publishing your books in paperback. Later in this book, I'll walk you through the steps to upload your book in both formats. And trust me when I tell you it's easier than you think!

When the paperback option was first introduced on Amazon, I dragged my feet for almost two years before I finally decided to publish in paperback. My hesitation meant I lost tens of thousands of dollars in royalties. I will not let you make the same mistake I did!

CHAPTER FOUR: THE WRITING & EDITING PROCESS

S o, you have the necessary equipment – a computer, internet access, and Microsoft Word - to self-publish a book on Amazon. You have looked over the book categories, likely seeing one or several that you are interested in writing in. You have also learned about the differences between publishing in Kindle and paperback, as well as the pros and cons of Kindle Select. You now know the basics of self-publishing, but here comes the hard part:

YOU NEED TO WRITE A BOOK!

Or you need to create a no or low-content book such as a journal, planner, notebook, or activity book. I'll be going over how to create low-content products later in this book. This chapter will deal with writing non-fiction and fiction books.

So, back to you writing your first fiction or non-fiction book.

How does one actually go about writing a book? Not just a book that you will enjoy reading, but one that millions of potential readers might buy. A book you can make money from.

Honestly, the process of writing a book is much harder than any of the other tasks involved with self-publishing. I have seen so many would-be authors fail even to start a single book because they allow the fear of the unknown and the fear of failure to overwhelm them. So many people claim they have a great book idea in their minds, but they never put pen to paper.

But you do not need to let this fear overwhelm you! Millions of people around the world are self-publishing books and making money from them, including me. There is no reason you cannot join us. You just need to write a book!

If you are like me, you may already have been writing your first book in your head before you even type a word of it out. I thought about my first book for weeks before sitting down to start writing it. But even if you haven't yet settled on an idea, you can still come up with a topic for a book.

While non-fiction topics have always come easily to me, fiction has come more organically. I often find myself just sitting down at the computer with no conceived plot. I let the story unfold before me with no idea who exactly the characters are or where the story is going. I just sit down and start writing. Maybe the story doesn't lead anywhere. Maybe it changes course. Maybe I hit a rode block and need to step away from the computer for a bit. But in the end, I just keep pushing myself to write, even if it's only a paragraph in a day.

Regardless of where you are in the thought process of writing a book, here are some tips and tricks that I find helpful in my writing process:

Brainstorm: Do you remember being in school and having the teacher tell you to brainstorm ideas, to just write down anything and everything that came into your head? I use this same technique today when I am writing my books. If you are entirely new to writing, or even if you are experienced but have writer's block, brainstorming can help.

I start with a topic, and then I just write down whatever pops into my brain, even if it does not make sense. I just keep writing down whatever I think of. I might brainstorm for just a minute or sometimes over an hour. I will just keep adding to my list until I am tapped out.

It is important to note that your brainstorming list is just a list; nothing you have on it is set in stone. As you continue with the writing process, you will likely add more things in and perhaps take some things out.

For example, when I write a book about reselling, I will brainstorm everything I want to cover in a particular book. I will just jot down whatever pops into my head. So, I may write down things like "account setup," "where to source," "photos," "customer service," etc. This is my time to try and figure out the main points I need to cover; some of these ideas might get crossed off, some might be combined, and others might be fleshed out. Again, these are just ideas, not the final product.

Sometimes brainstorming for one book leads to ideas for other books. This happens to me a lot when I am brainstorming fiction story ideas, as all kinds of potential plots will pop into my head. Again, I just write down whatever I think of, whether it relates to what I started brainstorming about or not. This usually means I am always left with lots of additional ideas that I want to turn into books.

Outline: After I finish brainstorming for a particular book, I start forming that list into an outline. I am sure you remember creating outlines in school, and I use the same basic format when outlining my books.

I start by dividing my brainstorming list into sections or chapters, and then under those sections, I put the topics that fall under them. I further draw out those topics with more bullet points until I have felt I have gotten most of the information down.

Using the reselling book example, I might take "photos" from my brainstorming list and decide that this would make for a good chapter. I will then figure out what I need to cover in the "photos" chapter, such as cameras, lighting, backdrops, angles, etc.

My fiction process works differently than non-fiction. With my non-fiction books, I need to provide a lot of statistical information and intricate details, so there is much more fact-checking and data that I need to research. However, fiction stories are entirely made up. The characters and the plot are all imagined in my mind. I typically outline just the main points I know I need to hit and then let the rest flow from there. So, while my non-fiction outline might be several pages, my fiction outline might only be a few lines.

As with the brainstorming process, your outline is not set in stone. An outline gives you a general idea of how your book will be laid out, but you can move things, add items, and take others out as you start writing. My books rarely follow my first outlines, but they help me get organized and begin writing.

Write: Once my outline is done, I start writing, fleshing out each section of my outline. One of the best pieces of advice I ever got about how to write was just to WRITE! Let the words flow, and do not worry about spelling, grammar, or sentence structure, as you can fix all those things later. Stopping to correct every misspelled word will interrupt your flow, and you will lose steam. As long as the words are coming to you, keep on writing!

Of course, you cannot write all day and night; you must take breaks. If you are on a hot streak, write for as long as you can. However, if you have writer's block, step away from the computer. Clear your head by doing something else, anything else. Go for a walk. Clean the house. Take a nap. Watch a movie. Forget about your book for a while, even for the rest of the day, so that you can return to it refreshed. Even if that means you do not get back to it for a few days or even a week.

That being said, don't take too long of a break. You don't want to lose interest in your own story. I often feel completely burned out from writing and tell myself I need a few weeks off, only to return to my book the next day. If the story is there, the words will eventually come.

If the words aren't coming, perhaps you need to change course with your story. Remember, this is YOUR book. If a character or plot isn't working, you can change either or both. Review your outline, if you made one, to remind yourself where you are going with your book. If you haven't started with an outline, you can still create one after you start writing. It may be easier to develop and outline after you have already written a few pages, as you likely have a better idea of the location, characters, and plot.

Depending on your book, the writing process could take days, weeks, or even years. Both my non-fiction and fiction books average around 45,000 words. Therefore, if I really apply myself, I can write the bulk of a book in a month by writing a couple of thousand words per day. If you are writing the next great American novel, your writing time will be much longer.

However, do not mistake quantity for quality. A book with a large word count does not mean it is any good; similarly, a short book lacking depth and information will not be met with favorable reviews, either. Focus on QUALITY, no matter how many words you write or pages you end up with. Quality always sells over quantity in the long term.

Story Structure: If you are writing fiction, you will eventually likely hear the terms **Pantsers** and **Plotters**. I had never heard these words until I started writing fiction, but they are common in the world of fiction authors.

Pantsers are writers who "fly by the seat of their pants." They do not plan out their stories; they just sit down and start writing, letting the story come to them. *Pantsers* give themselves the flexibility to see where the characters take them. They are not following an outline, so they do not feel pressured to keep storylines, so they do not pan out naturally.

However, with no plan, *pantsers* can find themselves getting stuck in their story, hitting more blocks than those who started with a plan. It can also be challenging for *pantsers* to stay focused on one book as their minds are constantly coming up with ideas for other books. Letting their minds ultimately lead them can backfire as they may struggle to focus on finishing a book.

Plotters follow the brainstorming and outlining we discussed earlier. I am a *plotter* as I figure out the basic structure of my books before I start writing them, although more so for my non-fiction books than my fiction books. Some *plotters* know precisely how their novels will unfold and typically do not deal with the type of writer's block *pantsers* as they stick to their outline.

However, *plotters* may find themselves feeling stuck with their original outline even when the story starts unfolding in a different direction. It can be challenging for them to switch things up even when the story itself is better navigating away from the original plan.

Plantsers are a combination of both. I, myself, feel like I am sometimes both a *pantser* and a *plotter* as I do brainstorm and outline my books, but I often do need to change course as the book naturally unfolds in another direction. I see myself as a *plotter* for non-fiction writing but have *pantser* tendencies when writing fiction.

Do not worry if you do not see yourself as a *pantser, plotter,* or *plantser*. I honestly think it is better not to label yourself as it is easy to then get stuck trying to fit into one mold. Many writers transform their writing styles the longer they write. The way I write books today is so much different than when I started, and my books are, in my humble opinion, much better than when I first started self-publishing. The most important thing is that you write your books. How you start and how you finish them is up to you.

The W Plot: An author friend taught me the **W Plot** method of writing fiction. The *W Plot* not only makes writing a fiction book easier, but the format is also what readers expect when reading fiction stories.

There are three acts in the *W Plot*: **Act I, Act II**, and **Act III**.

In **Act I**, you start the book with a **Trigger Event**, which immediately draws the reader in. You then set up the problem the character is facing. This act starts at a high and goes down to the lowest point, just as the first stroke of the letter W does. This low point is called the **1st Turning Point.**

Act II begins with the character **recovering from the problem** from *Act I*. The story arc is going up, just as the second stroke of the letter W does, finally reaching the top, where the **Second Triggering Even** occurs. The story arc goes back down, following the third stroke of the W letter. The **problem (trigger) deepens** and ends at the lowest point of the story.

Act III begins at the **2nd Turning Point** of the story and does up following the fourth and final stroke of the letter W. The **problem is resolving**, and the final point of the W is the **resolution of the story**.

If your book is part of a series, you'll want to wrap up the first part of your story but also leave the door open to the next book. This is called "happily ever after....for now."

You can, however, also end on a cliffhanger that you will continue in the second book. Cliffhangers are controversial. Some authors swear by them, while other authors avoid them at all costs. A good cliffhanger will lead readers to buy your second book. But they can also make readers very angry. They work, but they are risky.

My first fiction book ended with a cliffhanger, and I immediately received a negative review from a reader that was angry that the second book in the series wasn't immediately ready to read. If you are going to have your first book end in a cliffhanger, make sure the second book is already published or on pre-order and to be released in less than a month.

Edit: When I write a book, I write as much as possible without stopping to correct errors. However, this initial writing is just my first draft. It is common for my first draft to finish at 30,000 words, but then I begin my second draft and add another 10,000 to 20,000 words. My first draft is when I just write; my second draft is when I edit. Editing my second draft is my favorite part of writing a book.

This second draft is the longest part of the writing process for me, but I honestly find it easier than the first draft. Starting at the very beginning of the book, making corrections, and adding more text is less taxing than the first draft when it felt like I was typing non-stop with the achy wrists to show for it. My first drafts of non-fiction are also filled with stops and starts as I need to research facts. The second draft requires less research on my part, meaning I can write more from memory, which is easier.

Working through my second draft allows me to slow down my book writing process. After all, the bulk of the book is done in my first draft; I just need to fix things up in the second draft. And since I like to reach a specific word count, I can add additional text where needed. Editing is not just going back over my work and correcting grammatical errors; it is also examining how the book is laid out. I do not just fix misspelled words during the editing process; I work on the entire structure of the book.

Even though I typically start with an outline, I usually move sections of my books around during the editing process. Sometimes it is just paragraphs within a section; other times, it's entire chapters. Again, nothing is set in stone during the writing and editing process. There is nothing that cannot be fixed, deleted, or added. And even after I publish a book, I can still upload corrected files if a mistake is found later. Again, this is one of the best parts about self-publishing: you can always improve your work.

Another valuable tip I received about writing a book is that you should read it aloud as you edit it. Sure, you can silently read the words you have written as they appear on your computer screen to yourself in your head, but saying those words aloud is where you will catch the mistakes. I often look over the words I have written and see no errors. But when I read my writing back to myself aloud, I catch all kinds of mistakes.

You can have the program read your book aloud if you have Microsoft Word. Click on **Review** at the top of your Word document, then click on **Read Aloud Speech.** Highlight the first word you want the program to begin reading, and the feature will start. This allows you to listen to your work rather than read it, which is another great way to catch mistakes.

Working through my second draft takes me one to two weeks, depending on how much time I put into it daily. I typically work on my books for only an hour a day. At the end of my second draft, I am at the word count I want, although some words may be deleted and others added in the third draft.

For my third draft, I use the **Review: Spelling & Grammar** feature that is included in Microsoft Word to scan my document for errors. I then use **Grammarly Pro**, a paid feature that catches more errors than the standard Word program. Both editing features catch different issues within my writing. Some of their corrections I implement, while others I ignore. *Grammarly Pro* offers many more suggestions than Word, so while I can run the Word review in under an hour, it may take me a couple of days to work through *Grammarly Pro's* findings.

Finally, having someone else read your book before publishing it is always a good idea. In fact, it is helpful to have several people read it as no one person will ever catch every mistake. You can ask family and friends to proofread your work, and you can also hire a proofreader on websites such as Fiverr.com and UpWork.com. I have used both, but I prefer UpWork as the quality of work tends to be higher. Both sites allow you to post jobs or contact freelancers directly.

I pay upwards of $200 for someone on UpWork to proofread my non-fiction books and $100 for my fiction books. I pay more for non-fiction books as they require the proofreader to do extra fact-checking.

Font & Style: Amazon insists that you keep the font and style of your books simple. Not all fonts and styles translate to Kindle, meaning your book will end up looking like a mess once it is uploaded.

I use **Calibri (Body) 12** for my text and simple features such as **Bold**, **Italic**, and **bullet points**. I then choose **Heading 1** for my chapter headings; and **Subtitle** for, well, subtitles. I select **Open** under **Paragraph Spacing** and **12 pt spacing** between each paragraph. When it comes to self-publishing books, white space is commonly thought of as being preferred; and I have found that it works best for my non-fiction books as it breaks up the content and does not overwhelm the reader.

I use Bold or Italic to create separation and highlight specific passages. You can also use **Quotation Marks**, although I prefer the look of *Bold* or *Italic*. I bold all my chapters/sections and words and sentences I want to stand out. I use the **bullet** and **numbering** features within Word when creating lists.

The only other style feature I use is to **Center** headings; otherwise, my books are **Align Text Left**.

Page Breaks: Finally, you want to **add Page Breaks between chapters.** This feature is found under **Insert** at the top of every Word document.

To insert **Page Breaks**, you simply place your curser after the last word of what will end up being the previous page. Click on the **Insert tab** at the top of the page in Microsoft Word, and then click the **Page Break** icon. The text following where your curser is positioned will move down to a separate page. Continue going through your book and adding in page breaks where needed.

Note that you can undo page breaks simply by putting your curser next to the first letter of the text and hitting the **Backspace** key on your computer until the text goes back to the page it was originally on.

Page breaks give your Kindle book the look and feel of actual paper pages, breaking up the text so that it all does not run together. To get an idea of where your page breaks should be, look at an actual paper book. Note that the first pages – the title, author, copyright, and table of contents – are all on their own pages. Sometimes the chapter titles are on their own page, with the actual chapter contents starting on the next page. The formatting will transfer to both Kindle and paperback book files.

For my books, I insert a page break after the *Title* and *Author* page. The next page is the *Copyright*, and I insert another page break after that. I then include my *Table of Contents*, inserting a page break after that. Next comes my *Introduction*, followed by each chapter. Finally, I always have a *Conclusion* and *About the Author* page.

Your book is now written and the text formatted. Now you just need to create your Amazon account and format your files for upload, which we will cover in the following chapters.

CHAPTER FIVE:
HOW TO CREATE
YOUR AMAZON
KDP ACCOUNT

B efore you can upload your book to Amazon, you must create a KDP account, which you will remember stands for Kindle Direct Publishing. Whether it is a non-fiction, fiction, or low-content book, or if it is a Kindle or paperback, you only have one KDP account, which all the books you publish will fall under.

Note that you can only have ONE Amazon KDP account. According to their Terms & Conditions under 4.2:

Account Information; No Multiple Accounts. You must ensure that all information you provide in connection with establishing your Program account, such as your name, address, and email, is accurate when you provided it, and you must keep it up to date if you use the Program. You may maintain only one account at a time. If we terminate your account, you will not establish a new account. You will not use false identities or impersonate any other person or use a username or password you are not authorized to use. You authorize us, directly or through third parties, to make any inquiries we consider appropriate to verify account information you provide. You also consent to us sending you emails relating to the Program and other publishing opportunities from time to time.

4.3 goes on to state:

Account Security. You are solely responsible for safeguarding and maintaining the confidentiality of your account username and password and are responsible for all activities that occur under your account, whether you have authorized the activities. You may not permit any third party to use the Program through your account and will not use the account of any third party. You agree to immediately notify Amazon of any unauthorized use of your username, password, or account.

You will be prompted to agree to these Terms & Conditions when you create your Amazon KDP account, and understanding that you can only have ONE account is critical to keeping your account. Any attempts to create multiple accounts will result in you being permanently suspended from the KDP program.

Note that the account you use to shop on Amazon is a different account than that of your KDP account. So do not worry if you already have an account for buying, as that is entirely different than the one you need to self-publish books. However, if you already have an Amazon buyer's account, you will log in under that; but again, you are about to create a new account just for Kindle publishing.

Also, if you have an Amazon Seller Account and/or a Merch by Amazon account, your KDP account is a totally new account.

The program you will need to create an account in is called **Kindle Direct Publishing**; here is the link: **kdp.amazon.com/ signin.** Once on the KDP website, you simply click on the yellow **Get Started** button, which will take you to the account setup page.

Another note: Amazon calls its self-publishing platform KDP because, in the beginning, Kindle was the only format available. Now, however, paperback books are also included. The KDP name has not changed, but the formats available have.

The process of setting up my *Kindle Direct Publishing* account was the longest part of publishing my first book. There are several screens you will need to go through to fill in all your information, including your **Social Security number** (after all, if you are going to be making money with Kindle, you will owe taxes on that money) and your **bank account routing numbers** (so you can get your royalty payments directly deposited into your account every month).

Once you have completed the sign-up process, you will have access to your very own personalized *Kindle Direct Publishing* area. I have this page bookmarked so that I can easily access it throughout the day to monitor sales and pending uploads. There are four tabs at the top of your KDP account page:

- **Bookshelf**
- **Reports**
- **Community**
- **Marketing**

Bookshelf: Your *Bookshelf* is where all your books are located. You can choose for the system to show you ten books per page, twenty-five books per page, or fifty books per page. I currently have forty-six pages of books with the ten books per page option selected! You have editing features next to each of your books, which we will review in a bit.

Your *Bookshelf* is also where you upload new books. The top of the page reads **Create. Manage. Publish.** There is also a large **yellow + Create button.** Clicking on this button will open up a new page titled **What would you like to create?**

Here you can choose from the following:

- **Kindle eBook**
- **Paperback**
- **Series page**
- **Kindle Vella**

In this book, we will be focusing on the first two options: *Kindle eBook* and *Paperback*. However, I want to note the **Create and manage a** series link. Here you can link books in a series together, which makes it easy for readers to go from one book to the next. You can also **View existing series** to view all the titles in a series and edit series details.

We have already discussed how most books start with a Kindle version, and then a paperback version is added within the same listing. However, for print-on-demand planners, journals, and notebooks, which we will discuss in the last chapter of this book, publishers would only need to choose Paperback.

The main section of the *Bookshelf* is **Your Books,** where all your books are located.

You can **Sort by:**

- **Last modified**
- **Date submitted**
- **Title**
- **Contributor**
- **eBook price**
- **Paperback price**
- **Hardcover price**

You can **Filter by:**

- **All:** All your books under all pen names
- **Draft:** Unpublished books
- **In Review:** Books that Amazon is reviewing
- **Publishing:** Books that have passed Amazon's review process and are uploaded to the system
- **Live:** Books that are live on Amazon's website

- **Blocked:** A book you or Amazon has made unavailable to edit or publish

You can check the box to **View titles in series.** This will show you all of the books you have in a series. Note that there is a **Manage series** button available for each book.

There is also a **Search** feature on the *Bookshelf* page where you can quickly locate a book by title or pen name. I use this feature often to narrow down my fiction books from my non-fiction titles.

Reports: I spend a lot of time in the Reports section of my KDP account; after all, that is where I can see how much money I am making! In late 2022, Amazon updated the Reports section. Clicking on Reports will now bring up the following tabs:

- **Dashboard**
- **Orders**
- **KNEP Read**
- **Month-to-Date**
- **Promotions**
- **Pre-orders**
- **Royalties Estimator**
- **Kindle Vella Dashboard**

Dashboard: Here, you can choose the following default options, which also coordinate with the tabs at the top of the page.

- **Today's estimated royalties:** Clicking on *View Royalties Estimator* will take you to a new page where you can filter the data for dates, pen names, and even book titles to see your royalties for years, months, and even certain days.
- **Today's orders:** Clicking on *View Orders* will take you to a new page where you can filter the data for pen names, books, marketplaces, formats, and prices.
- **Today's KENP Read:** Clicking on *View KENP Read* will open up the full *Kindle Edition Normalized Pages Read,*

which will show you the page reads for the books you have enrolled in Kindle Select.

- **Today's top-earning books**
- **Top formats (current month)**
- **Top marketplaces (current month)**

Community: The next tab at the top of your KDP account page is *Community.* Here, you can find announcements from Amazon and forums for publishers to ask questions for other publishers to answer. As with many online communities, the forums can be a bit harsh to newcomers. However, you can learn a lot just by reading the posts.

More helpful than the forums, I feel, is the actual Amazon **HELP** section, which is linked at the top of the *Community* page. Here you can find in-depth answers to any account questions you may have. This page has an in-depth database of tutorials and user guides available for every section of the KDP site.

Contact Us: Also, under the *Help* tab within the *Community* section is the *Contact Us* link, which is at the bottom left-hand side of the page. Like most *Contact Us* features on large websites, Amazon will first try to narrow down your question to send you to a page that answers it.

However, almost all questions will eventually lead you to a section where you can either send an email or call to speak to someone in person. Like most call centers, email and telephone options are often answered in a country other than yours. If you cannot communicate with a telephone representative effectively, try the email option.

Marketing: The fourth and final tab at the top of your KDP account page is *Marketing.* Here you can perform several tasks under **Marketing Resources:**

KDP Select: You can enroll an eBook into KDP select within the actual book listing under *Bookshelf,* or you can do it here. The nice thing about this section is that Amazon will show you all the books that are not enrolled but are eligible.

Amazon Ads: You can access the *Amazon Advertising* portal here or directly once you have set up your account. I have an entire *Amazon Advertising* chapter coming up later in this book.

Author Central: You can access *Author Central* here or directly once you have set up your page. *Author Central* is a dedicated page where you can view your books, sales ranks, and customer reviews from one single portal. If you have multiple pen names, you can easily toggle back and forth between them. To be honest, the only information I use this page for is to easily view my books' sales ranks.

A+ Content: A new feature under the *Marketing* tab is *A+ Content*, which Amazon says allows you to add images, text, and comparison tables to your product detail page to engage readers and give more information as they consider buying your book. This link leads you to an entirely new page with tutorials on creating these features in your product pages. This is advanced content and something you should only explore once you are firmly established in your self-publishing career.

Run a Price Promotion: Here is where, if your Kindle eBook is enrolled in Kindle Select, you can create **Kindle Countdown Deals** and **Free Book Promotions**. You can also create these offers directly within your book's listing on the *Bookshelf* page by choosing **Promote and Advertise** under **Kindle eBook Actions.** We already discussed these special offers in *Chapter Three* under the *Kindle Unlimited* section.

Nominate your eBooks: Amazon frequently runs contests for authors, as well as including them in special promotions. You can **Nominate a book for a Kindle Deal,** which are limited-time discounts offered on select eBooks. You can also **Nominate a book for Prime Reading**, where Amazon offers a rotating selection of eBooks available to Prime Members to read for free. Note that this section is currently in Beta testing and may not be available to all publishers.

More Marketing Resources: Here, you can learn more about Kindle Pre-Order, Gifting for Kindle, and Kindle Instant Book Previews.

ROYALTIES: In my opinion, getting paid is the best part of self-publishing! There is nothing better than tracking sales of your books, watching the numbers grow, and seeing your royalties increase. However, how and when you get paid can be a bit confusing when you are just starting out with KDP.

I spend most of my time in the **Reports** section of my KDP account, where the royalties information is located.

First, the money you make from your books is called **Royalties**. Amazon offers publishers two different royalty rates, which we have already discussed earlier in this book. But to refresh, you can choose a 35% royalty rate or a 70% royalty rate for Kindle eBooks. Amazon keeps 40% for paperback books, paying you 60% of the book's sale price AFTER they take out the cost to print the book. Hence, you must charge more for a paperback copy of your book to make the same amount of money as the Kindle version. There is no printing cost for eBooks, after all.

Amazon distributes your book royalty income two months AFTER the month in which you earned those royalties. For example, my first month selling books on Amazon was in December 2013. However, I did not receive the money I earned in December 2013 until February 2014. The money I earned in January 2014 was not sent to me until March 2014.

You must have $100 in your KDP account to be issued payment. So, if you start self-publishing books in June but only earn $99 in June, you will NOT get paid in August. Instead, your royalties from June will carry over into July. If you sell $100 worth of books in July, the $99 from June will be added to the $100 from July; you will then receive a payment of $199 in September. While it can be frustrating to have to wait so long to get paid, once you are selling books and continuing to upload new titles, the money will start to grow, hopefully resulting in larger payments as the months go on.

Amazon usually distributes royalties to authors' bank accounts on the last day of the month, although it can vary daily. Amazon also distributes royalties from each country separately. I never get one single deposit of royalties; I get several. Sometimes they are all deposited on the same day; other times, a few countries lag a day or two behind. As a general rule of thumb, you can look forward to being paid within the last few days of the month.

Amazon issues KDP payments via direct deposit into your bank account, which is why you need to provide bank routing numbers when you sign up for an account. Depending on your country and what bank you are using, the transfer of funds can take as little as one day but up to a week in some cases. Since I am in the United States and use a U.S. bank, my money always clears within one day.

CHAPTER SIX: HOW TO FORMAT BOOK FILES FOR UPLOAD

There are several different ways to format your book files and prepare them to be uploaded into Amazon's system. You can format your document in Word, your document in Kindle Create, your document using Vellum, or you can pay someone to format your book for you. I personally use Kindle Create, but I will be discussing all four options in this chapter.

Formatting In Word: Once your book document is finished and the page matter itself is formatted (bold, italics, centering, page breaks, etc.), you can upload it directly to Amazon in a Word-supported format, in this case, a **Web Page Filtered** document.

Up until now, as you have been writing and editing your book, you have been saving it as a regular Microsoft Word document. However, for it to be uploaded onto KDP directly from Word, it must be saved as a *Web Page Filtered* document. This will change the document from a **.DOC** to a **.DOCX**. And it is in this format that you can then upload the file to Amazon.

To save your book as a *Web Page Filtered* document, click on **File** in the top left-hand corner of the screen and select the **Save**

As option. Likely up until now, you have been choosing *Save* or clicking on the *computer disk icon.* Selecting *Save As* will bring up a window for you to choose where on your computer you want to save the document (such as to your *Desktop* or into a specific folder). And it will allow you to change the file type to a *Web Page Filtered* document that ends in *.DOCX.*

Note that your book will also be saved as a regular Word document. Wherever you are saving your files will now show TWO copies of your book, one as *Microsoft Word .DOC* and one as *Web Page Filtered .DOCX.* You can easily go back into your *Microsoft Word .DOC* copy, make changes, and then resave it as a *Web Page Filtered* document, overriding the first save.

I am constantly editing and updating my books, which is another huge bonus of self-publishing. Even after my book is on the Amazon site and selling, I can change the book files on my computer and upload new copies whenever I want to.

I have three folders on my desktop, one for each of my pen names. Within each of these folders are individual folders for each book where I save the book covers (for Kindle and paperback, as well as any of the graphics purchased to make them), the original Microsoft Word *.DOC* files, and the most current Web Page Filtered *.DOCX* files. This system helps me keep all my books and their files neatly organized on my computer to access them when needed quickly. I also save these files to an external hard drive; for added measure, I even email myself copies of these files. These files are my livelihood, so I can never play it too safe when ensuring I have them backed up.

Format In Kindle Create: The second option, and the one I use, for formatting your books, is to use **Kindle Create**, which is Amazon's free book formatting software. *Kindle Create* is free to download for both PC and Mac computers. And despite its name, it formats your book for both Kindle and paperback.

You will find the link to download *Kindle Create* at the top of your *Kindle Direct Publishing* account page. I have my copy saved to my desktop for easy access. This software updates periodically; Amazon will prompt you when a new version is available.

After you have downloaded *Kindle Create* and are ready to format your book, you simply click on the Kindle Create icon on your computer to open the program up. Once the program is open, you will click on the **+ Create New** and then click on the **Choose** button. This will open a new screen where you can **Choose File** (.DOC, DOCX) from your computer. All you need to do is select your .docx book file and wait a few minutes for it to upload fully.

From here, *Kindle Create* will import your book file into their program and will walk you step-by-step through the formatting process. Note that this book conversion turns your Word document into both a Kindle formatted eBook and into a 6x9-inch paperback formatted book.

Kindle Create will offer you several optional features to implement into your book, such as making your *Table of Contents* clickable, allowing readers to be taken directly to specific chapters rather than turning the pages manually. *Kindle Create* also allows you to format your **Chapter Titles**, **Chapter Subtitles**, and **Chapter First Paragraph** (where you can make the first letter of each chapter paragraph larger than the other characters.)

You can add other details, such as **Subheadings, Block Quotes, Poem Formatting, Separators, Opening Quotes**, and **Opening Quote Credits**. I encourage you to play around with each of these extra features to see how or even if they would benefit your book. You can easily undo any of these options; do not worry; nothing is set in stone.

You can save your book anytime in *Kindle Create* and come back to make changes later. And when you have your final version ready, you simply click on the **Publish** icon at the top of the page, and your converted copy will be saved both within *Kindle Create* and onto your computer wherever you choose.

You can create new versions of your book anytime you want to, so do not worry if you hit the *Publish* icon and then realize you need to make some corrections. This happens to me all the time! I typically have three different versions before I get to the final one I upload to Amazon. And even then, if I create another new version, Amazon makes it easy to upload a new file at any time. Remember, your book files on Amazon are not permanent; you can always make changes and upload new files to replace the old ones anytime you want to.

Format In Vellum: A popular book formatting program in the author community is **Vellum**, which is available for purchase at **Vellum.com**. *Vellum* packages start at $199.99, so it is a hefty investment. However, *Vellum* offers advanced features that *Kindle Create* does not, including:

- Custom Drop Caps
- Ornamental Flourishes
- Box Sets
- Advance Copies
- Links for Social Media
- Store Links
- Formatting for Apple, Kobo, etc.

Paying Someone to Format Your Book: If formatting your Kindle eBooks and paperback books yourself feels too overwhelming, you can hire someone to do the work for you. For years, I hired contractors on *Fiverr.com* to format my Kindle books for me. For $5, I was able to have my book formatted and ready for upload to Amazon. You can also hire people to format books on *UpWork.com*.

It was not until I started publishing my books in paperback that I downloaded *Kindle Create* to format my books myself. Doing my own formatting allows me more freedom to make changes to my files. However, if you are just starting out self-publishing books and are feeling the pressure of publishing your first book, there is absolutely nothing wrong with paying someone a few dollars to do it for you.

Some tips to consider if you do hire someone through *Fiverr* or *UpWork*:

- Both sites allow you to post jobs or browse service postings.
- Look at the seller's feedback before ordering.
- Make sure you read exactly what the seller is offering before ordering.
- Note things like the number of revisions they offer in case you need something changed.
- That being said, if you are only paying $5 to $10, do not take advantage of a seller by demanding constant revisions (you get what you pay for).
- More experienced sellers charge more than new users as new users are anxious to build up their portfolio by taking low-paying jobs.
- Both sites offer you the option to tip workers extra after they have completed their job
- Both sites allow you to rate sellers.
- Sellers can also rate customers, so if you treat a seller poorly, you will also get a negative review, which may make future sellers unwilling to accept a job from you.

Converting my Word document into a format I could upload to Amazon was something that held me back from self-publishing. I was convinced that the process was too complex for me. Hopefully, I have shown you that it really is quite simple. Whether you choose to do it yourself or pay someone to do it for you, formatting your book file is one of the easiest parts of self-publishing and one that I am now embarrassed to admit I was ever scared of.

CHAPTER SEVEN: HOW TO UPLOAD BOOKS TO AMAZON

N ow comes the part that, if you are like I was, you are dreading: uploading your book onto Amazon. If just the thought of this process scares you, rest assured that it did me, too. In fact, I was so overwhelmed by the prospect of publishing my book on the Amazon site that I almost gave up before I even started writing. I was so sure that the whole thing would be too complicated that I would not be able to do it. But I was so wrong!

The truth is that uploading your book to Amazon is the easiest part of self-publishing your book in both Kindle eBook and paperback book format. It is easier than writing the book, easier than formatting the book, and easier than promoting the book. Once you have created your KDP account, it literally takes just a few minutes to upload your book for sale.

To upload your book to Amazon, log into your KDP account. After you sign in, you will be on your personal KDP page. At the top of the page are the following tabs:

- **Bookshelf**

- **Reports**
- **Community**
- **Marketing**

The page defaults to your *Bookshelf*, which is perfect as this is also the page where you upload new books.

In large type, you will see **Create. Manage. Publish.**

Below that text is a field titled **UPDATED Create a new title or series**. Amazon revamped this section in mid-2022 to make the process a bit more streamlined. Here Amazon tells you that you can, *Reach readers in the format they want. You can now publish an eBook, paperback, hardcover book, or Kindle Vella story. If publishing a series, you can create an Amazon series page and add your books.*

Let's begin with uploading a Kindle book.

Click on the yellow + Create button.

A new page will open titled **What would you like to create?**

In the Kindle eBook square, click on the yellow Create eBook button.

Ac new screen will be brought up containing three separate pages. The first one is titled **Kindle eBook Details,** and there are several sections here to complete.

Language: The first field is *Language*, and this will default to the language of the Amazon site you are registered under. If you are publishing in America, this will default to English. You can also publish books in:

- Afrikaans
- Alsatian
- Arabic (Kindle only)
- Basque
- Bokmål Norwegian
- Breton

- Catalan
- Chinese (Kindle only)
- Cornish
- Corsican
- Danish
- Dutch/Flemish
- Eastern Frisian
- Finnish
- French
- Frisian
- German
- Gujarati (Kindle only)
- Hebrew (paperback only)
- Hindi (Kindle only)
- Icelandic
- Irish
- Italian
- Japanese (Kindle only)
- Latin (paperback only)
- Luxembourgish
- Malayalam (Kindle only)
- Marathi (Kindle only)
- Manx
- Northern Frisian
- Norwegian
- Nynorsk Norwegian
- Portuguese
- Provencal
- Romansh
- Scots
- Scottish Gaelic
- Spanish
- Swedish
- Tamil (Kindle only)
- Welsh
- Yiddish (paperback only)

As you continue your self-publishing journey, you may find it advantageous to publish your books in several languages. For instance, while English is the official language of the United States, Spanish is spoken by a large part of the population. And those Spanish speakers are using Amazon's American site to shop, including for books written in Spanish. You can hire people to translate your books into different languages on *Fiverr.com* and *UpWork.com*.

Book Title: The following field is *Book Title.* Here you will need to provide your main book title and *Subtitle*, if you have one. It is important to note that while you can change your Kindle book titles at any time after your book has been published, you cannot change your paperback book titles.

In addition, your paperback book title and subtitle must match your cover design exactly; otherwise, Amazon will not publish your book. However, these do not have to match up with the Kindle versions of your books. While you have flexibility in your Kindle book titles, you do not have the same option for your paperback books. And since you want your Kindle and paperback books to match, you want to take the time to get your titles and subtitles right.

If you have ever shopped for books on Amazon, you have likely noticed that many book titles are incredibly long. That is because self-published authors like to cram as many keywords into their titles, specifically their subtitles, as possible. This is a workable strategy for Kindle eBooks but does not work well for paperbacks because your titles must match the text on your paperback covers.

When creating your titles and subtitles, it is essential to try to work keywords in where possible. This is especially true for non-fiction and print-on-demand products such as planners, journals, and notebooks. This book, for instance, probably would not sell well if it was simply titled "Amazon KDP." I had to add descriptive words I know Amazon customers will search for.

Amazon provides the following "Title Do's & Don'ts":

- Do enter your title name exactly as it reads on the cover of your book
- Do ensure that your title is exactly the same for both your Kindle and paperback versions, as this is how they are linked together on one detailed page
- Do not add anything from the following list of prohibited items in the title field:
- Unauthorized reference to other titles or authors
- Unauthorized reference to a trademarked term
- Reference to sales rank (e.g., "bestselling")
- Reference to advertisements or promotions (e.g., "free")
- Only punctuation (e.g., "!!!!!!!!")
- Using only "unknown", "n/a", "na", "blank", "none", "null", "not applicable"

Amazon also provides this guidance for subtitles:

- A subtitle is an optional secondary title that contains additional information about the content of your book. Together, your title and subtitle must be 200 characters or less. Your subtitle should adhere to the same guidelines as your title above. What is an example subtitle? Mary Shelley gave her most famous novel the title "Frankenstein," with the subtitle "The Modern Prometheus." Her book can be called and is recognizable by both names. Using the subtitle "The Modern Prometheus," she references the Greek Titan as a hint of the novel's themes.

Series: If your book is part of a series (for instance, I group my business books by year), you can add series details so readers can easily find your other titles on one detail page. You can add the title you are uploading to an existing series or create a new one. Linked formats for the title you are uploading will automatically be added to the series once the setup is complete.

Amazon provides the following guidance in regards to adding books to a series:

- *Ensure your series is complete by adding all the books in the series. You can only manage the books in your KDP account. This helps readers buy a complete series and navigate from one book to the next.*
- *Include books in your series that share common characteristics, such as characters, a setting, or chronology. This helps readers understand what to expect from your series by grouping your related titles together.*
- *If you have different formats of a book, link them together in your Bookshelf and then add either format to your series. Any linked format will automatically be added to your series. This allows readers to see all available formats for your series titles on one page and select the format that works best for them.*
- *If you have series titles in multiple languages, create separate series for each language to help readers easily find all the titles in your series in each language.*
- *Avoid adding duplicate content to the same series to ensure readers purchasing all the titles in your series are receiving unique content.*
- *When you create a series, you will be creating a Reading Order for your readers. Your titles can be numbered to be read in linear order or Unordered to be read in any order.*
  Edition Number: The next field, Edition Number, is optional. You can provide an edition number if your title is the first edition of your book or if it is a new edition of an existing book. For example, when you first publish a book, that copy is a first edition. But if later you correct a few mistakes and upload a new version in place of the first version, the new copy is a second edition.

Author: Here is where you enter the **First Name** and **Last Name** of the **Primary Author or Contributor**. So, you will either be entering in your own legal name or a pen name. Note that this field cannot be changed once your book is published on Kindle or paperback. This is the one field that is set in stone for both formats. Amazon will also use these names to create your *Author Pages, Series Pages, etc.*

Note that the paperback book setup page allows you to enter a *middle name/initial, prefix, and/or suffix* to your author's name. The Kindle book page does not. However, you can contact Amazon directly if you wish to have these additions made to your Kindle author name.

Contributors: If you have anyone else contribute to your book, you can add their names under the *Contributors* section. You can add:

- Author
- Editor
- Forward
- Illustrator
- Introduction
- Narrator
- Photographer
- Preface
- Translator

Note that if you are the author of your book, you only need to enter your name in the *Author* section, not again under *Contributors.*

Description: One of the most important sections of your book's detail page is the *Description.* Here you want to summarize your book in a way that will prompt customers to purchase it. You can enter HTML code here or use Amazon's features to add:

- **Bold**
- **Italic**
- **Underline**
- **Numbers**
- **Bullets**

- **Paragraphs**

Amazon offers the following suggestions for writing your book descriptions:

Keep it simple: *Describe the main plot, theme, or idea only. Avoid details that may overwhelm or confuse a reader who is only taking a second or two to decide whether to find out more about your book. Also, keep your language short and simple. Aim for a 150-word paragraph with sentences that are easy to scan.*

Make it compelling: *Avoiding overwhelming and confusing details will help make your description compelling, but also consider how to grab readers' attention. For example, write a first sentence that draws them in. This sentence may be a reader's first impression, so make it memorable. Also, set expectations by showing what genre your book belongs to.*

Keep it professional: *Again, this might be your reader's first impression, so make sure your description is polished--no misspellings or grammatical errors. It may be hard to edit a text you have looked at several times, so show it to others to get a fresh set of eyes.*

Amazon also advises KDP users of the following book description restrictions:

- Pornographic, obscene, or offensive content
- Phone numbers, physical mail addresses, email addresses, or website URLs
- Reviews, quotes, or testimonials
- Requests for customer reviews
- Advertisements, watermarks on images or videos, or promotional material
- Time-sensitive information (for example, dates of promotional tours, seminars, or lectures)
- Availability, price, alternative ordering information (for example, links to other websites for placing orders)

- Spoiler information for Books, Music, Video, or DVD (BMVD) listings
- Any keywords or book tags phrases

A self-publishing secret that Amazon does not tell you but that all profitable authors know is that you want to load your description up with as many keywords as possible. Just as you want to add keywords to your book's title and subtitle to help customers find your book when they are searching on Amazon's site, keywords in the description will also help your book be discovered.

However, you do not want to just add a long line of keywords; you want to work them into sentences. For instance, keywords that will help readers find my Ebay books include:

- Ebay
- Home-based business
- Make money online
- Work from home
- Reselling

But instead of just listing those words, I would put them in a sentence, such as, "Looking for a home-based business that allows you to make money online and work from home? Then reselling on Ebay might be for you!"

Amazon provides a section for keywords, which we will go over shortly, but it is important to work keywords into your title and your description so that customers have the best chance of finding your book.

Note that the first four lines of your book's description are what customers will see when they click on your book. They will have to click on the read more link to bring up the rest of your description. So those four lines are critical to getting potential customers to learn more about your book and possibly purchase it. Your first sentence or two can make or break a sale, so really sell it and dress it up with a bold font. Check out some of the books on the best-seller lists that are in your same category for inspiration.

Publishing Rights: You have two options to choose from in this section:

- **I own the copyright, and I hold the necessary publishing rights** (choose this option if your book is under copyright and you hold the necessary rights for the content being published); OR
- **This is a public domain work** (if you are translating a book that is already available for free from Amazon).

If you wrote your book yourself, then you will choose the first option. Under U.S. copyright law, your self-published work is protected as soon as you put pen to paper. Copyright is based on your creative authorship and is not dependent on any formal agreement with a publisher or self-publishing company. However, registration with the U.S. Copyright Office is beneficial.

In other words, if you thought your story up and wrote it down, even if it is unpublished, it is yours alone. No one else can publish your work. This is also a caution to you against plagiarizing another writer's work.

Keywords: As I have already touched on, keywords are a huge part of getting customers to find your books on Amazon, which is why you want to add them to your *Titles* and in your book *Description*. However, Amazon also allows you to select up to seven search keywords that describe your book.

Note the part that reads: *up to seven*. This is where self-published authors do things a bit differently; instead of just putting in seven individual words into the seven slots Amazon provides, you want to load up the spaces with as many keywords and phrases as possible.

Let's again use one of my Ebay books as an example. Instead

of putting one keyword or phrase in each field (Ebay, reselling, home-based business), I would put as many keywords as I can, even if the keyword phrases do not make sense in some places. A look at one of the keyword fields for an Ebay book might read: *Ebay reselling guide book home-based business idea*

So how do you know the best keywords to use? I know my keywords due to my years of experience, but you may need to do some research when you are just starting out. First, brainstorm keyword ideas; then test these keywords on Amazon's website to see if they bring up books like yours. This will give you a good starting point to narrow down your list.

There are also KDP keyword generator websites where, for a fee, you can pay for access to their keyword generators. **PublisherRocket.com** is the software I use; not only does it help with keywords for my book listings, but it also generates keywords for ad campaigns, which we will discuss later in this book.

A Google search for a "KDP keyword generator" will bring up a huge list of results; most charge a fee and/or require you to sign up for an email list where they will try to sell you other services. **Kindlerander.com** is a popular option as it allows you three free searches per day or $7.99 for 24-hour access. Since you are likely only searching for one book at a time, the free version of three searches per day should be enough when you are just starting out.

Amazon offers the following advice for entering keywords:

- *Combine keywords in the most logical order. Customers search for "military science fiction" but probably not for "fiction science military."*
- *Use up to seven keywords or short phrases. Keep an eye on the character limit in the text field.*
- *Before publishing, search using keywords you are considering on Amazon. If you get irrelevant or*

unsatisfying results, make some changes. When searching, look at the suggestions that appear in the "Search" field drop-down.

- *Think like a reader. Imagine how you would search if you were a customer.*

Amazon suggests the following as useful keyword types:

- *Setting (Colonial America)*
- *Character types (single dad, veteran)*
- *Character roles (strong female lead)*
- *Plot themes (coming of age, forgiveness)*
- *Story tone (dystopian, feel-good)*
- *Amazon advises on keywords to avoid*
- *Information covered elsewhere in your book's metadata (title, contributors, etc.)*
- *Subjective claims about quality (e.g., "best novel ever")*
- *Time-sensitive statements ("new," "on sale," "available now")*
- *Information common to most items in the category ("book")*
- *Spelling errors*
- *Variants of spacing, punctuation, capitalization, and pluralization ("80GB" and "80 GB," "computer" and "computers", etc.).* **Exception:** *Words translated in more than one way (e.g., "Mao Zedong," or "Mao Tse-tung," "Hanukkah," or "Chanukah."*
- *Anything misrepresentative, like the name of an author not associated with your book. This kind of information can create a confusing customer experience. Kindle Direct Publishing has a zero-tolerance policy for metadata that is meant to advertise, promote, or mislead*
- *Quotation marks in search terms. Single words work better than phrases, and specific words work better than general ones. If you enter "complex, suspenseful whodunit," only people who type all those words will find your book. For better results, enter this: complex, suspenseful whodunit.*

> *Customers can search for any of those words and find your book*

- *Amazon program names like "Kindle Unlimited" or "KDP Select."*

Amazon also offers these other metadata and keyword tips:

- *Customers are more likely to skim past long titles (over 60 characters)*
- *Focus your book's description on the book's content*
- *Make sure your book's metadata adheres to KDP's eBook and paperback guidelines*
- *Your keywords can capture useful, relevant information that will not fit in your title and description (setting, character, plot, theme, etc.)*
- *You can change keywords and descriptions as often as you like*
- *If your book is available in different formats (physical, audio), keep your keywords and description consistent across formats*
- *On Amazon, use the menu on the left to brainstorm keyword ideas. For example, in the Romance category, you can refine search results in the menu on the left by "Romantic Heroes," such as Vikings or doctors. If your book is a Viking romance, consider using "Vikings" as a keyword.*

Categories: Almost as important as your title, description, and keywords are the categories you choose to put your book in. As we discussed earlier in this book, you can select two categories for both your Kindle eBook version and your paperback book version. However, once your book is published, you can contact Amazon and ask them to add each version of your book to up to eight additional categories.

Remember, too, that the categories differ for Kindle eBooks and paperback books. This gives you an advantage as you can choose different categories for each version of your book, not just within each listing but also when you ask Amazon to add more for you. That means you could have your book in up to sixteen different categories, which will go a long way for more readers to find your books.

In Chapter Two, I wrote out the instructions for how you can contact Amazon to have them put your book into additional categories. I'm adding the steps here again for your convenience:

How to contact Amazon to add your book to additional categories: I am including this section both here as well as later on in this book since it is so important to the process. Adding your books into multiple categories is key in helping sell books.

Amazon doesn't make contacting them easy. They would prefer to send you to articles on the site that will likely solve your problem. But in the case of wanting to add your book to additional categories, you need to message them directly.

From **Amazon Author Central** or when logged into your **Kindle Direct Publishing** page, look for the **Help** link at the top of either page.

You will be taken to a new page with a list of **HELP TOPICS** on the right.

The last line on this list is **Contact Us.**

Click on *Contact Us.* You will be taken to a new page titled **How can we help?**

Select **Amazon Book Page**.

And then select **Update Amazon categories.**

A **contact form** will then appear for you to fill out. You will need to provide the following:

- **Format:** ASIN or ISBN =
- **Marketplace:** The Amazon site your book is for sale on. In America, this would be .com.
- **Book format:** Kindle or paperback

- **Category:** Using this book, *Beginner's Guide To Amazon KDP*, as an example, I would type in *Kindle Store: Kindle eBooks: Business & Money: Industries: E-commerce: Auctions & Small Business* (this is the main category the Kindle version of this book is in)

I would then repeat the *Category* section for the additional categories I want Amazon to manually list my Kindle book.

After clicking **Send message**, I would then create another request form for the paperback version of the book.

Back on the main listing page under *Categories*, there are two more sections to complete.

Age and Grade Range: This is an optional section, and it is typically for those publishing children's books, as parents can sort books by age. If you publish books for kids, you can select an age range minimum and a US grade range minimum. If you are writing books for adults, you can bypass this section. I personally never edit this section.

Pre-order: Pre-orders are standard for fiction writers as they build a fan base eager to buy their next release. I do not do pre-orders for my non-fiction books, but I do for my fiction books, especially for books in a series, as I want the readers of the first book to go ahead and pre-order the second book. Some authors load several books to Amazon as pre-orders in a series, especially if they release new books every month or two. If your books are linked together as a series, Amazon will automatically alert a reader of the next book in the series, whether it is on pre-order or already live.

Select either

- **I am ready to release my book now** OR
- **Make my Kindle eBook available for Pre-order**

You cannot put paperback books up for pre-order. If you are offering both a Kindle and paperback version of your book, make sure to upload the paperback version a few days before the Kindle version is scheduled to go live, as it takes Amazon longer to approve paperback books. Ideally, you want both editions to be released simultaneously, but Amazon currently makes that impossible. Sometimes, they approve paperback books overnight; other times, it takes them days.

End of Page One: Once you finish this first page of KDP, you can **Save as Draft** or **Save and Continue**. *Save and Continue* will move you onto the second page of your book's upload. Note, however, that you can go back and change most of this information before you publish your book. Not every field can be changed after publication; however, as we have discussed, you can change Kindle book titles but not paperback. And you can never change the author's name you entered on either version.

Manuscript: On the second page, the first field is for Manuscript. Here is where you will do two things:

Digital Rights Management: Here, you can choose to enable DRM on your Kindle book. According to Amazon:

DRM (Digital Rights Management) is intended to inhibit unauthorized distribution of the Kindle file of your book. Some authors want to encourage readers to share their work, and choose not to have DRM applied to their book. If you choose DRM, customers will still be able to lend the book to another user for a short period, and can also purchase the book as a gift for another user from the Kindle store. Important: Once you publish your book, you cannot change its DRM setting.

I personally choose *NO* here as I want people to buy my books, not read them for free by borrowing them from someone else. Most self-published authors also choose NO for DRM.

Upload Book Manuscript: Here is where you upload your book's file. You either created your file in Word and saved it as a .DOCX file, used Kindle Create, used Vellum, or had someone create your file for you. Whichever method you used, now you simply click on the yellow button and select the file from your computer.

Remember that you can upload a new version of your book anytime.

If Amazon detects a **spelling error** in your manuscript file, an alert will show here. You can click on the possible spelling error to see if it is actually a misspelled word or perhaps slang you used that Amazon does not recognize. If it is a legitimate error, you can fix it in your Word document, reformat the file in Kindle Create, and upload the new file. If the word is not a spelling error, you simply click the *Ignore* button.

Kindle eBook Cover: The next field is for you to upload your book's cover. I have an entire chapter ahead that is devoted to making covers. Amazon offers you two options in this section:

- **Launch Cover Creator** to make your book cover (you can use Amazon's templates or upload your own image, which you can then lay text over); OR
- **Upload a cover you already have** (JPG/TIFF only).

Again, I will cover these options more in-depth later in this book; but for now, remember that it is in this section where you will upload your cover file. You will need to upload all of your files before moving on to the third and final page of the listing form.

Kindle eBook Preview: Once your manuscript and cover have been processed, you will need to click on **Launch Previewer** to approve the files. Note that sometimes it can take a while for Amazon to process these files; after my files are uploaded, I usually just click *Save As Draft* and return to it after an hour or so.

Kindle eBook ISBN: The final section on this page allows you to enter an **ISBN** for your book. Note that Kindle eBooks do not require an *ISBN*, but it is something to consider purchasing.

Paperback books DO require an *ISBN*.

According to Amazon:

An ISBN is an International Standard Book Number. You can publish your book without one, but if you do have one, you may enter it here. However, it will only be used as a reference and will not actually appear on the detail page of your eBook (only the ASIN will). Important: Do not use an ISBN from a print edition for your digital edition. If you want to include an ISBN for the digital version of your book, it must be a unique ISBN. You can purchase an ISBN from multiple sources on the Web.

Most self-publishing websites, including Amazon, will offer you a **free ISBN** for your books. However, you can **purchase your ISBNs on the website Bowker.com.** Now, *ISBN*s are expensive; I buy 100 of them at a time for $500. But purchasing my *ISBN*s outright ensures I have complete control over my books.

When I first started self-publishing, I did choose the free options from Amazon for my books. However, I now purchase my own for my non-fiction and fiction books. Paying for your ISBNs is especially important if you plan to self-publish books on websites other than Amazon.

However, if you plan only to publish short Kindle eBooks and make your money from Kindle Select page reads, it is not as important for you to own the ISBNs. Also, it isn't necessary to include ISBNs for no-and-low content books such as planners, journals, notebooks, and activity books.

But if you see yourself publishing books on other websites, and certainly if you plan on publishing paperback books, then buying ISBNs is something you need to consider. As a business expense, you can claim the cost on your taxes.

Do not use the same ISBN for both the eBook and paperback versions of the same title. eBook ISBNs must be unique to eBook versions. According to Amazon,

An ISBN is required to publish your paperback. All ISBNs assigned after 2007 are 13 digits. You can choose to use a free ISBN from KDP or to provide your own. The free ISBN from KDP can only be used on KDP for distribution to Amazon and its distributors. It cannot be used with another publisher or self-publishing service. If you use your own ISBN to publish your paperback, you can use that ISBN to publish your book elsewhere.

Publisher: Next, there is an optional field to enter a **Publisher**. I just put whatever author name I use for the book I publish, whether it is my name or one of my pen names. However, this field is optional.

Once you have approved your book and cover files, you can **Save and Continue** onto the third and final page. Again, you can change the information on this page, including the book files, at any time.

KDP Select Enrollment: At the top of the third and final page is **KDP Select Enrollment.** One of the biggest decisions you will make when publishing your Kindle books to Amazon is whether to enroll them in *Kindle Select*, which is Amazon's *Kindle Unlimited* program.

I have already covered the *KDP Select* program earlier in this book, but here is a brief recap:

Amazon customers can pay a monthly subscription fee to enroll in **Kindle Unlimited**, which allows them to borrow as many eligible Kindle books as they want. The key word here is *eligible* as an author must voluntarily enroll a book into the program to make it available for *Kindle Unlimited* subscribers to read for free. It is rare that a traditionally published book is enrolled in *KDP Select*; the eligible books are almost all self-published.

Amazon collects the *Kindle Unlimited* subscription fees and divides the revenue among the authors whose books were downloaded under the *KDP Select* program. As of this writing, the payout is around half a cent per page read; or one penny for every two pages read. Amazon counts page-read as a Kindle page being physically turned by the reader; the days of customers skipping to the end of the book and the author being paid for all pages is over.

Publishers can enroll their Kindle books in *KDP Select* for 90 days. You can choose to renew automatically or turn off the automatic renewal option and choose to manually re-enroll. Enrolling in *KDP Select* has three distinct features tied to it:

- The opportunity to **make money from page reads,** not just sales
- The opportunity to run **Free Books Promotions** (five free days per book per each 90-day enrollment period)
- The opportunity to run **Kindle Countdown Deals** (five per book per each 90-day enrollment period for books priced between $2.99 and $24.99)

When you are just starting self-publishing, enrolling your books in *KDP Select* can be beneficial. When it comes to fiction specifically, it is tough for new authors to get noticed. Therefore, enrolling fiction books into *KDP Select* will allow Amazon customers to test out books from new authors without buying them.

When *KDP Select* was introduced, I enrolled all my books in the program. However, today, none of my non-fiction books are enrolled. I have built up my brand as a business author over the years, and now customers are willing to buy my books outright.

However, I do have my fiction books enrolled in *KDP Select*. Since I have just started publishing fiction and am still learning the craft, my fiction income comes primarily from page reads. As I build my library and gain more readers, I may eventually take my fiction books out of *KDP Select*; but for now, I am content with earning money from the page reads.

Note that if you enroll your Kindle book in *KDP Select,* you must remain exclusive to Amazon during the 90-day enrollment period. That means you cannot publish the eBook version of your book on other distribution sites such as Draft2Digital or IngramSpark (more on these two companies later). However, you can publish the paperback version of your book on other sites. Only the eBook version of your book must be exclusive to Amazon under the *KDP Select* program.

Territories: The next section of the page is **Territories**. According to Amazon:

*If you are sure you have all rights necessary to make this title available worldwide, choose **All territories (worldwide rights)**. This will allow customers from around the world to purchase your title on Amazon.com, Amazon.co.uk, Amazon.de, Amazon.fr, Amazon.es, Amazon.it, Amazon.co.jp, Amazon.com.br, Amazon.com.mx, Amazon.com.au, Amazon.ca, Amazon.nl, and Amazon.in. If your book is your original content and you've never published it before, you most likely have worldwide rights.*

*If you don't hold worldwide rights to sell and distribute your title, choose **Individual territories**. Then, indicate the territories in which you hold rights. This will limit sales of your publication to the selected territories only.*

Here is the list of territories included in each Kindle Store:

- US Kindle Store: United States
- UK Kindle Store: United Kingdom (including Guernsey, Isle of Man, Ireland, Gibraltar, and Jersey)
- DE Kindle Store: Austria, Germany, Liechtenstein, Luxembourg, and Switzerland
- FR Kindle Store: France, Monaco, Belgium, Switzerland, and Luxembourg
- ES Kindle Store: Andorra, Spain
- IT Kindle Store: Italy, San Marino, Vatican City, and Switzerland
- JP Kindle Store: Japan
- NL Kindle Store: Netherlands
- BR Kindle Store: Brazil

- MX Kindle Store: Mexico
- CA Kindle Store: Canada
- IN Kindle Store: India
- AU Kindle Store: Australia, New Zealand

Customers located in the available territories not listed above can purchase your book from the US Kindle Store or Amazon.com. The period of copyright protection varies among countries and regions, so ensure that you indicate your territory rights accurately for public domain works. If you are updating an existing title's territory rights, remember to publish your changes by clicking the *Publish Your Kindle eBook* button at the bottom of the page.

All the legal talk from Amazon is overwhelming, I know. But the bottom line is that if you hold the rights to your book, i.e., you wrote it yourself, then you can click on **All territories (worldwide rights).**

Primary Marketplace: This section is easy; simply choose the website where you expect most of your books to sell. The selection will default to the country you created your account in. If you are in the United States, this will be Amazon.com.

Pricing, royalty, and distribution: Next up is the **Pricing, royalty, and distribution** section. Also known as "how you will make money"! I will discuss pricing your books in depth in an upcoming chapter, but I'll touch on the main points here.

Authors have flexibility in pricing their books, and Amazon pays us differently depending on whether a customer buys or borrows our book. Amazon offers two different payouts, or **royalty**, options for Kindle eBooks that are purchased:

- **35% payout** for books priced 99 cents to $2.98 and books priced $10 or more. Note that no delivery fee applies when you choose the 35% payout option. However, this is best for books under $2.99 or books with very large file sizes. OR

- **70% payout** for books priced from $2.99 to $9.99. This is the price range for the majority of Kindle eBooks on Amazon. A delivery fee is attached to the 70% payout option, which is 15 cents per megabyte.

Most authors choose the 70% royalty payment. Most eBooks are priced from $2.99 to $9.99, so to be competitive, it is important to price your book in this range. While you can typically charge more for non-fiction books, fiction, which is a highly competitive genre, usually means books are priced lower to attract readers. However, there are far more fiction readers than non-fiction customers.

Fiction is a volume business. If someone enjoys one of your fiction books, they are likely to purchase more, if not all, of your fiction books. If you have ten books priced at $2.99, depending on the file size, you could earn $2.10 for each book someone buys. If one customer buys one of each of your books, you will profit $21.

However, if you have a multitude of non-fiction books as I do, likely, most customers will only buy one or two of your books, depending on the topic. I earn roughly $7 for each of my non-fiction Kindle eBooks. With fiction, you have a better chance of bringing in multiple sales from the same customer. So, while you earn less per book with fiction, you typically earn more overall compared to non-fiction.

Amazon will automatically convert the price of your book for international distribution. You can compare your cut of the royalties using the chart shown in the **Pricing, royalty, and distribution section.**

Just as your book files can be changed at any time, so can your pricing. You may start a book at $2.99 in hopes that you will attract customers, but then raise it if your book is getting a lot of sales. I used to price my Kindle books at $2.99 each and enrolled them in *KDP Select*. However, now that I have made my non-fiction books longer, most Kindle versions are priced at $9.99 and are not enrolled in *KDP Select.*

Note that unlike *KDP Select*, where authors only get paid per page a reader views, when a customer outright purchases a book on Amazon, the author gets paid regardless of whether the customer ever reads it. I still have page-read royalties coming in from people who downloaded my books years earlier when they were still in *KDP Select.*

You may want to try launching it at 99-cents under the 30% royalty level for your first book. Remember that there is a lot of competition on Amazon and that you will need reviews for your book to sell. Setting the price at 99-cents will hopefully encourage some sales, bringing in needed reviews. Again, you can change your price at any time, so as your book begins to sell more copies, you can raise the price.

Unless you already have a large social media following, I strongly suggest that you enroll your first book in *KDP Select* and allow it to be borrowed by those with *Kindle Unlimited* memberships. Again, while you will only make a penny per every two pages read, letting your book be borrowed will hopefully generate reviews and can help with your book's rank. As a new author, you may initially only have people borrow your book, not buy it. Again, you need your first readers to leave you reviews for your book to generate future sales. And since *KDP Select* is only a 90-day commitment, you can always pull it out of the program later.

Oh, and about getting your readers to leave you those reviews? Simply ASK THEM! A friendly note at the end of the book asking for them to leave you a review, along with a link to your Amazon author page, is an easy way to encourage readers to hopefully give your book four or more stars, along with a nice write-up. Amazon also prompts readers to leave a review and automatically directs the reader to the book's detail page.

However, many authors like to include the personal ask.

While my non-fiction books are priced higher and are not enrolled in KDP Select, my fiction books are. I like to offer free book promotions on my fiction titles to improve their rank and to get readers to join my mailing list. I will discuss this form of promotion later in this book.

Many new authors are offended by the idea of selling their books for so little money and try to start out asking $20 or more. Again, remember that the Kindle market is very, very crowded. Hundreds of thousands of other self-published authors are trying to sell their books, many of whom have been at it for years. I have been selling Kindle eBooks since 2013 and have sold thousands of copies. It took years before I could justify selling my Kindle eBooks for $9.99.

Book Lending: The second to last section is for Book Lending. Per Amazon,

The Kindle Book Lending feature allows users to lend digital books they have purchased through the Kindle Store to their friends and family. Each book may be lent once for a duration of 14 days and will not be readable by the lender during the loan period. Lending is only available for Kindle books purchased on Amazon.com.

If you have purchased a copy of your own book, you are welcome to lend it. However, you can only lend a title once per the terms of the Kindle Book Lending program. Loans of Kindle books are not purchases and thus are not eligible to receive royalty payments.

All KDP titles are enrolled in lending by default. For titles in the 35% royalty option, you may choose to opt-out of lending by deselecting the checkbox under "Book Lending" in the book pricing & promotion section of the title setup process. Still, you may not choose to opt-out of a 70% royalty optioned title or a title included in the lending program of another sales or distribution channel.

I no longer allow the lending of my books. I initially did, but book lending is not as popular as it once was. I would rather have a reader borrow a book under *KDP Select* or buy it outright so that I can make money on it.

Pre-order Terms: The very last field you must read is **Terms & Conditions**. The link to the current terms is active in this section. You will need to click on the link and agree to the terms to proceed with publishing your eBook.

Publish Your Kindle eBook: Once you are comfortable that all your sections have been filled out correctly, it is time to publish your Kindle eBook! You do this by clicking on the orange **Publish Your Kindle eBook** button at the bottom of the page. It can take Amazon up to 72 hours for your Kindle eBook to be live on their website. And, again, you can make changes to most of the fields after publication.

If you are putting your book up for pre-order, the yellow button will read Submit for Pre-order.

Paperback Books: The process for creating a paperback version of your book is much the same as when you uploaded the Kindle version. Once your Kindle eBook has been published, the book will show up on the *Bookshelf* on your KDP account page. Simply click on the **+ Create paperback** link to get started.

If you are uploading a paperback-only book, such as low-content journals, planners, notebooks, or activity books, you will start on the main page of your *Kindle Direct Publishing* account. Under *Create. Manage. Publish.* is a field titled **UPDATED Create a new title or series.** Click on the **yellow + Create** button. You will be taken to a page titled **What would you like to create?** Click on the yellow **Create paperback** button.

If you have already uploaded a Kindle version of the book you now want to create a paperback version for, some of the fields will automatically be pre-filled for you. However, you can edit most of these if you so desire. The fields that are pre-filled include:

- Language
- Book Title
- Subtitle
- Series
- Edition Number
- Author
- Contributors
- Description
- Publishing Rights
- Keywords
- Categories

Adult Content: It is not until you get to the bottom of the first page that you will encounter a field that is different from the Kindle page, and that is **Adult Content.** Here you will be asked, *Does this book contain language, situations, or images inappropriate for children under 18 years of age?* You then select NO or YES. Unless the book you are publishing is specifically geared toward children, I recommend selecting NO.

After clicking on the **Save & Continue** icon at the bottom of page one, you will be taken to the second page of your paperback book details.

Print ISBN: Unlike eBooks, which do not require an ISBN, printed books do. As I discussed earlier, you can purchase ISBNs on **Bowker.com.** Or you can choose for Amazon to assign you a free KDP ISBN. If you can afford it, I recommend you purchase your own, although, in my early days of self-publishing, I did use the free ones that Amazon provided. I use the free ISBNs Amazon offers for my no-and-low content books.

If you purchase your ISBN from Bowker, you will enter *Bowker* in the **Imprint field.**

Publication Date: If you have previously published your book on another website, you will enter the date on which your book was first published. However, if you publish your book for the first time, you can skip this section as the date will automatically fill in when your book goes live on Amazon's website. As I've already mentioned, you can not submit paperback books for pre-order. Only Kindle books have a pre-order option.

Print Options: Unlike eBooks, paperback books have numerous options for the page interiors. Amazon offers the following Ink and Paper Types:

- **Black and white interior with cream paper** (typical for fiction and memoirs; paper weight is 55 pounds)
- **Black and white interior with white paper** (this is Amazon's default selection and the one most authors, including myself, use; typical for nonfiction with a paper weight of 55 pounds)
- **Standard color interior with white paper** (the more affordable option for books with color, although not recommended for books with full-color page elements; paper weight of 55 pounds)
- **Premium color interior with white paper** (for books with full-color elements such as illustrations, graphics, and images; paper weight of 60 pounds)

Trim Size: Another difference between Kindle eBooks and paperback books is **Trim Size**. When you are publishing a tangible book with actual paper pages, you need to select exactly what size the pages will be.

Most fiction and non-fiction self-published paperback books on Amazon are 6x9 inches. However, Amazon offers several different sizes. Sizes such as 7x10, for instance, are great for journals, while 8.5x11 is what most notebooks are sized at. Children's books are also sized larger than 6x9. We will talk more about *Trim Sizes* in the print-on-demand chapter at the end of this book.

Bleed Settings: According to Amazon,

Setting your interior to "bleed" allows printing at or off the edge of a page. It is used to support images and illustrations. Most books use "no bleed" unless there is a specific reason to apply "bleed." Changing the bleed settings will not change the manufacturing cost.

For books created in Microsoft Word, Kindle Create, or Vellum, I choose *No Bleed*. For my print-on-demand products, such as planners, journals, and notebooks, which I will talk about in the last chapter of this book, I choose Bleed (PDF only) as they are, in fact, PDF files.

For my **fiction and non-fiction books**, I typically choose the default option of a **Black & white interior with white paper, the 6x9 in trim size, No Bleed,** and a **Glossy** cover.

For my **no-and-low content books,** I create books in various sizes but typically choose the default option of a **Black & White interior with white paper, Bleed, and** a **Glossy** cover.

Paperback cover finish: According to Amazon,

*Our covers are printed on 80# (220 GSM) white paper stock with either glossy or matte finish. **Glossy** finish is shiny. It makes black covers darker and artwork more striking. It is typical for textbooks, children's books, and nonfiction. **Matte** finish has minimal sheen and a subtle, polished look. It is typical for novels and other fiction.*

I used to choose *Matte* for all my paperback book covers, regardless of genre or size. However, I am now choosing *Glossy* finish for all of my book covers as the matte finish is prone to showing fingerprints. However, you can choose whichever you like, and, like almost everything else, you can change your settings even after your book is published.

Manuscript: Here is where you will upload your paperback book file. Amazon supports the following formats for paperback books:

- PDF
- DOC
- DOCX

- HTML
- RTF

I use the file created using **Kindle Create** for both my eBook and paperback interiors. However, when I am uploading print-on-demand products, I upload PDF files that I create using special software. Again, I will talk about this more in the last chapter of the book.

Book Cover: Next up is the section where you can either create a book cover using Amazon's **Cover Creator**, or you can upload your own print-ready PDF file. We will be discussing book covers in the next chapter. Just note that your paperback book cover differs from your Kindle version, as your paperback cover also includes a spine and a back cover. Kindle eBooks only require a front cover.

Launch Preview: Once both your paperback book manuscript and your cover are uploaded, you will click on the **Launch Previewer** button. Just as it does with Kindle files, it can take Amazon a while to process these uploads and make them ready for you to preview. I save my work and come back to this page after an hour or so. Note that you will not be able to move on to the final page until you have previewed and accepted your book's complete file.

Once you have approved your book's file (Amazon will show you the cover and interior pages put together as they will be printed), the final section on the second page of your book listing is the **Summary.** Here Amazon will show you **Your Printing Cost.** Remember that the cost to print your book will automatically be deducted from the sale price of your book.

You can click **Save & Continue** to proceed to the third and final page of the listing section.

Territories: On the third and final page of uploading your paperback book, the first section is **Territories**. This is the same as when you uploaded the Kindle version of your book, so you can refer to it earlier in this chapter if you want a refresher. However, I always choose **All territories (worldwide rights).**

Primary marketplace: Another field that is the same as it was for the Kindle version is the **Primary marketplace**. This will default to the country you are uploading from. In the case of the United States, the default will be Amazon.com.

Pricing, royalty, and distribution: This section is set up just as it was for the Kindle version of your book. However, the royalty amounts are different between eBooks and paperback books. On Amazon, publishers earn a 60% royalty on paperback books. In addition to paying Amazon a cut of the book's purchase price, the printing cost is also taken out of the book's purchase price.

For example, I have print-on-demand journals priced at $11.95. Amazon takes $2.34 to print these books and then their cut of the royalties, leaving me with a 60% royalty payout of $4.83.

Note that the cost to print a book varies due to page numbers and trim size. The longer and larger a book, the more it will cost to print.

Amazon will automatically match the price you set for your book for international buyers. However, unlike Kindle eBooks, paperback books are not as widely distributed. As of this writing, most of my non-fiction and fiction paperback books are only available to customers in the United States and Great Britain on Amazon's website.

After you have set your paperback book's price, you are ready to click on the **Publish Your Paperback Book** button at the bottom of the page. Unlike Kindle eBooks, which Amazon typically approves in under a day, it can take Amazon several days to approve paperback books. I have had to wait up to a week for a paperback to be approved. This is because Amazon thoroughly checks paperback books to ensure they will print correctly when ordered.

Request Proof Copies: After your paperback book has been successfully published on Amazon's website, you can request proof copies at a discounted rate. For instance, I can buy one of the print-on-demand journals I referenced earlier for $2.34 plus shipping.

However, I order my books directly from the Amazon website rather than order author-proof copies. Why? Well, for one, it will help my author rank. Ordering proof copies of books does not show up in your sales or rank. I would rather pay a few dollars more for my book and benefit from the listing having a sale. Plus, I will earn 60% of the royalties from the sale, which ends up making my purchased copy cost almost the exact cost as a proof copy.

CHAPTER EIGHT: HOW TO CREATE BOOK COVERS

I am sure you have heard the saying, "You can't judge a book by its cover." But when it comes to selling books on Amazon, customers can and do decide whether they will even click on your book to learn more about it based on your cover. A cover is just as important, sometimes arguably more important than the content of your book.

There are three ways you can create both Kindle and paperback book covers:

1. Design your own book covers using graphic design software
2. Design your own book covers using Amazon's Cover Creator
3. Hire someone to design your book covers

I have utilized all three of these options in my self-publishing career so that I can break down the pros and cons of each. However, a few things first about book covers on Amazon.

Kindle eBook covers, according to Amazon, must meet the

following specifications:

- Kindle eBooks must have a marketing cover image provided for use on the website detail page. This is provided separately from the eBook file.
- The ideal size of your eBook cover art is a height/width ratio of 1.6:1. This means that for every 1,000 pixels in width, the image should be 1,600 pixels in height.
- To ensure the best quality for your image, particularly on high-definition devices, the height of the image should be at least 2,500 pixels.
- **Ideal dimensions for cover files are 2,560 x 1,600 pixels.**
- The minimum image size allowed is 1,000 x 625 pixels.
- The maximum image size allowed is 10,000 x 10,000 pixels.
- The image file size should be 50MB or smaller.

Amazon also offers the following instructions:

If the marketing cover image size is smaller than the 2560 x 1600 recommendation, a reminder message is displayed at time of upload. Covers with less than 500 pixels on the shortest side are not displayed on the website. If your cover image is smaller than the recommended size, Amazon strongly recommends that you create a new image that meets the size requirements. Do not stretch the image to meet the size requirements because this may lower the image quality.

Cover art with white or very light backgrounds can seem to disappear against the white background. Try adding a narrow (3-4 pixel) border in medium gray to define the boundaries of the cover.

The content of the cover image must not:

- Infringe another publisher's or artist's copyright on the same cover
- Mention pricing or other temporary promotional offers

Paperback book covers are different from Kindle eBook covers as the file you upload must contain the back cover, spine, and front cover in one single PDF image. The size of the image will depend on the number of pages in your book as well as the trim size.

Amazon supplies a free **Paperback file setup calculator** that you can download to give you the margins, bleed, and spine requirements for paperback books. Amazon also offers several cover templates that you can download. To access these resources, click on the **Community** tab at the top of your KDP account page. Then click on the **Help** tab at the top of the page. Then click on the **Book Formatting** links on the left-hand column.

Design your own book cover using graphic design software: I make most of my book covers myself using design software and graphics subscriptions. Let's talk about design software first.

To design a book cover, you need a graphic design program, a program where you lay out the size of your book and then add graphics and text to it to create a cover. There are many available, including the following user-friendly options:

- Adobe Photoshop (plans start at $29.99 per month)
- Canva (plans start at $119.99 per year)
- Crello (plans start at $7.99 per month)
- Easil (plans start at $6.25 per month)
- Design Wizard (plans start at $7.42 per month)
- Keynote (available in the Apple Store)
- PowerPoint (available with Microsoft Office Suite)
- Snappa (plans start at $10 per month)
- Stencil (plans start at $9 per month)
- Visme (plans start at $15 per month)

Adobe and Canva are wildly considered the two most popular graphic design options for creating book covers. With any design program, however, what you are looking to do is to enter in the size of your book cover and then add in graphic elements, usually from another source.

There are many graphics websites where you can purchase commercial photos and images, including:

- **Canva Pro:** Not only can you use Canva to design covers, but if you have a Pro membership, you can use their graphics on print-on-demand products, including your book covers.
- **Creative Fabrica:** An excellent source for fonts, graphics, and even POD templates. All-access plans are $29 per month.
- **Pixabay:** Royalty-free vector graphics and images. Be sure to double-check each potential graphic to ensure you can use it for commercial use.
- **Shutterstock:** The number one website for purchasing photographs for book covers. Subscriptions start at $29 per month.

I am currently designing my book covers using *Canva* and importing commercial graphics and photos from websites such as *Shutterstock* and *Creative Fabrica.* If you are new to graphic design, note that most of these websites offer video tutorials for users. And you can also find videos on YouTube that will walk you through the book cover creation process using whichever products and sites you want.

When I create a cover, I start with the Kindle version first. Using Amazon's recommended sizes, I open up Canva and enter in the dimensions. This brings up a page with the cover dimensions. I can use the fonts and colors provided within Canva and some of the basic shapes they provide. As I pay for the Canva Pro membership, I can also use their graphics in my designs.

When you place a graphic on a book cover and then sell that book, you must have print-on-demand or commercial rights for that graphic. I pay for those graphics with my *Canva, Shutterstock, Creative Fabrica,* and other subscriptions.

Once I have my Kindle cover designed, I make a copy of the image and change the dimensions for the paperback version. For the paperback book, I need to provide Amazon with one complete cover file that includes the front page, spine, and back page.

Once my covers are designed, I save copies to my desktop, where I can then upload them to Amazon. I save the Kindle covers as .JPG files and the paperback covers as .PNG files.

Design your own book cover using Amazon's Cover Creator: If designing your own book cover using graphic design software and purchasing commercial use graphics seems too much, there is another option within Amazon itself.

After uploading a book manuscript to your KDP account, the next section is the Book Cover. Here you can upload a cover file that is already done (by you or someone you hired), or you can use **Amazon's Cover Creator.**

If you click on the **Launch Cover Creator** button, a new window will open where you are given three choices from which to select an image:

- **From Image Gallery:** This will lead you to Amazon's Image Gallery, which they boast contains thousands of graphics for your book cover. Unfortunately, the images are not that good and have already been used numerous times by other publishers. The best options here are under the *Art Paper* section, which offers colors and patterns but not photos. You can then choose from one of several pre-determined layouts. Your book's title will automatically be imported to the cover and spine. You can change colors and fonts, and you can add text to the back cover. This is an okay option for technical books that do not need an elaborate cover design to sell.
- **From My Computer:** If you have a Kindle eBook cover

already designed but need a paperback version, you can use this option. This will place your Kindle cover on a paperback book cover. The drawback here is that sizing tends to be an issue, with the Kindle cover usually being a bit smaller than needed, creating black space on the sides. Plus, the system wants to force you to use their text, which will then cover your graphic. You can delete their text, but unfortunately, this also means that no text will appear on the spine. And having your author's name and book title on the spine is expected from readers. Your other option here is to import just an image or photograph that you have purchased the commercial use for and see how Amazon lays it out on a cover.

- **Skip This Step:** If you are still in the development process for your book's cover, Amazon will provide a placeholder image. Some authors choose this option for books they want to have on pre-order but have not designed a cover for yet. I personally would not publish a book, even on pre-order, without a cover, but if you are an established author, this may be something you can get away with while you wait for your final cover to be ready.

Hire someone to design your covers: If you are entirely new to graphic design, explicitly creating book covers, it is perfectly acceptable to hire a designer to create your book covers. In fact, in the self-publishing world, most people hire someone to create their book covers. A good book cover designer understands the different genres and how to design covers to attract readers.

While I design some of my book covers, I also hire professionals for some of my books, specifically fiction. I use two websites to find book designers: **Fiverr.com** and **UpWork.com.**

Both *Fiverr* and *UpWork* allow you to post jobs for freelancers to apply for, and they also offer the option to contact sellers directly about jobs. Freelancers on both sites can post the "gigs" they have for sale, complete with their resumes and examples of their work.

A simple search of "book cover designer" on either side will bring up hundreds of potential freelancers. You can then narrow down your search using various filters such as experience, location, language, rating, etc.

I have both posted jobs for designers to apply to and contacted designers directly about jobs. In my experience, *UpWork* is great for posting jobs for designers to apply to. Regarding *Fiverr*, I have had much better luck browsing through the available gigs myself.

When hiring someone on *Fiverr* or *UpWork*, I look for the following:

- **Positive feedback from past customers.** Customers can rate sellers on both sites, so read reviews before you hire anyone.
- **Portfolio of completed cover designs.** Make sure the designer you hire has experience creating book covers in your genre. You do not want to hire someone to design a romance book cover, for example, who has only ever created covers for cookbooks.
- **Fluent English speakers**. You can narrow down your search for those fluent in whatever language you want. Many sellers, especially on Fiverr, are in Asia, and it can be challenging to communicate with them if they are not fluent in English.
- **At least two revisions.** It is highly unlikely that the first cover design you are given will be exactly what you are looking for, so it is expected that the seller will allow for revisions.

You will find beginner, intermediate, and expert cover designers on both sites, and how much they charge will reflect on their experience. However, new designers are always trying to get their foot in the door and will offer their services for a lot less to gain job experience. I have had some of my best covers done by those new on the sites as they were eager to gain reviews.

Of the two, you will typically get a better-quality product, albeit for more money, on *UpWork*. But it is worth looking around on both sites to get a feel of how book cover designers work and the types of cover designs that are available. Note that both sites offer the option of "tipping" after a job is completed; if the person you hire does a good job, it is good practice to tip them after the project is complete.

A good book cover needs to do two things simultaneously: Stand out from the crowd while also fitting in with the genre. Accomplishing both is challenging, so hiring a professional is a good investment.

CHAPTER NINE: HOW TO PRICE YOUR BOOKS

I've already touched on book pricing several times in this book, but in this chapter, I'll discuss it more in-depth. How you price your books isn't just about how much money you will make but also about getting customers to buy your books in the first place.

Books that are priced too low can be seen as being of poor quality. Books that are priced too high will turn off buyers. Finding the sweet spot is a delicate balance of ensuring you are charging what your book is worthwhile and attracting the largest customer base possible.

I'll be dividing my pricing advice into the three main genres of books:

- **Fiction**
- **Non-Fiction**
- **Low Content**

Pricing Fiction Books: Writing fiction is a labor of love. Authors pour their hearts and souls into their characters, crafting intricate worlds and stories. When a writer finishes a fiction novel, they are often completely physically and emotionally spent. But the hope is there that readers will find their book and fall in love with it. And the big dreamers see television and movie deals awaiting them as their book gains traction.

Hundreds of millions of people around the world love to read fiction. Certainly, a loving crafted product that is in demand warrants a high price. Right?

Well, not when it comes to fiction books, unfortunately. Whether they are traditionally published or self-published on Amazon, most fiction book prices are pretty low, with the prices dropping the longer the books are out. The $19.99 hardcover from a best-selling author soon drops to $9.99 and then $6.99 in paperback. The eBook might end up selling for only a dollar or two. Even if the book is later adapted to the small or big screen, the original book price is rather small as the book is rereleased in mass paperback form.

And for self-published authors? Well, you aren't going to be able to price your first fiction book for $20 or even $10. In reality, if you want to build an audience and make money, your first books won't make much money.

For self-published fiction books on Amazon, you'll want to enroll your first books in *Kindle Select* so that *Kindle Unlimited* subscribers can read them for "free." You will earn a small cut of the *Kindle Unlimited* membership fees that are pooled together and divided among Amazon and authors. And I mean a small cut; the current payout for *Kindle Unlimited* page reads is one cent for every TWO pages. Yup, if you enroll your book in *Kindle Select*, you will only early half a cent per page that is read.

Some people will hopefully buy your book outright, enabling you to earn 70% of the royalties. But at the average selling price of $2.99, that means you will earn around $2 for every sale of your book. And getting sales is hard when you are just starting out, meaning you will rely on *Kindle Unlimited* subscribers to borrow your book. In these early days, it's more about building an audience, getting your book higher in the rankings, and hopefully getting good reviews.

Money? Well, with any luck, that will come later down the road.

So why are fiction books priced so low? And how does anyone make money writing fiction books?

Fiction is the most popular genre of books. There are hundreds of different troupes within the fiction category, and self-published authors are continuously feeding more and more books into the pipeline for readers to devour.

And avid fiction readers are ferocious readers. Some claim they read a book a day. Yes, you read that right: one book per day! And it is self-published books that allow them to do so as self-published books are typically shorter than traditionally published books and are released much faster.

A traditionally published romance novel, for instance, averages around 80,000 words. Historical fiction and fantasy series easily top 100,000 words. These types of books take days for even the most die-hard readers to finish.

Compare those word counts for self-published books, which can be as short as 30,000 words to qualify as a full-length book. Amazon also has short story categories where books are around 10,000 words. Readers can finish several self-published books in less time than they can read a traditionally published novel.

And since most indie authors focus on specific troupes, they attract an audience that wants very specific storylines. Nicholas Sparks writes gut-wrenching romance novels. But romance readers, especially those with *Kindle Unlimited* subscriptions, are looking for niche romance.

We discussed troupes at the beginning of this book regarding figuring out which category you want to write in. Let's take another look at romance troupes that are popular right now on Amazon to give you a better idea of what readers are looking for.

When you look at the available Kindle book categories, there are numerous sub-categories under *Romance*. In addition to these sub-categories, you can also narrow *Romantic heroes:*

- Alpha Males
- BBW
- Bikers
- Cowboys
- Criminals & Outlaws
- Doctors
- Firefighters
- Highlanders
- Pirates
- Royalty & Aristocrats
- Spies
- Vikings
- Wealthy.

You can also choose *Romantic themes:*

- Amnesia
- Beaches
- International
- Love Triangle
- Medical
- Second Chances
- Secret Baby
- Vacation
- Wedding
- Workplace

To get an example to show you, on August 31, 2022, I clicked on *Alpha Males* under *Romantic heroes*. The book in the number one position was *The Do-Over (The Miles High Club Book 4)* by TL Swan. The Kindle version of the book was priced at $3.99.

However, the book was enrolled in *Kindle Select,* meaning *Kindle Unlimited* members could read it for free as part of their paid membership. The author then earned one penny per every two pages read. At 553 pages, this is a much larger book than other books in the same genre. And they earned around $2.75 for every Kindle book sold.

You may think that poor TL Swan isn't making much with this book, as regardless of whether customers buy her book or read it as part of Kindle Unlimited, her royalty cut doesn't amount to much.

Well, *The Do-Over* alone makes TL Swan over $28,000 a month! By adding all of her titles, she is making well over six monthly figures. That's well over one million dollars a year. And almost all of her books are enrolled in *Kindle Select*, meaning most of her income comes from *Kindle Unlimited* page reads.

Not bad for a low-price book that many people are reading for "free," huh?

Now, TL Swan has spent a lot of time crafting her books and writing to market. She gives readers books that feature alpha males, a popular troupe on Amazon. She doesn't have to hand over most profits to a publishing house. She earns 70% for each Kindle book she sells, and even though the *Kindle Unlimited* payout is small, so many people read her books that it all adds up.

Could she make this kind of money writing non-fiction? No. Could she have worked to this level of income had she started trying to sell books for $10 or more? No. Would she make this kind of money if she had a contract with a traditional publishing house? No, because traditional publishing houses are producing alpha male hero books.

Indie authors such as TL Swan make money with fiction books they write to market and price right. Not too low, as potential readers might think the book is poor quality. But not too high that those without a *Kindle Unlimited* subscription wouldn't purchase it.

Fiction is largely a volume game. The reader base is huge, meaning there are never enough books for them to read. Therefore, authors can write shorter books and price them lower, making up for the difference in the number of books sold and pages read.

You may have noticed that many Kindle eBooks are priced at least $2.99. **Amazon has two different price structures for Kindle eBooks:**

- 35% royalties for books priced between 99 cents and $2.98; or $10 or more
- 70% royalties for books priced between $2.99 and $9.99.

Why does Amazon have two royalty structures? The answer is a mix between profit margins and perception. Let me explain:

Amazon keeps 30% off the profits from every Kindle book sold on their site if it is priced between $2.99 and $9.99. So when a book sells for $3, Amazon keeps around $1 (more or less depending on the file size). Amazon keeps 65% of the profits from every Kindle book sold on their site if it is priced from 99 cents to $2.98. So when a book sells for 99 cents, Amazon keeps around 65 cents (more or less, depending on the file size).

I should note here that Amazon does charge authors a 15-cent per megabyte fee on Kindle files. The larger your book file, the more of a cut Amazon will take from your royalties.

For books enrolled in *Kindle Select,* Amazon pools all of the money it makes from *Kindle Unlimited* subscriptions and, after taking their own cut of the profits, divides the profits among sellers whose books are enrolled in the program and whose books had page reads that month.

But the main reason Amazon likes books priced between $2.99 and $9.99 is customer preference. Buyers like low-priced books.

Not too low, as again, they could signal low-quality. But lower than traditionally published paperback and hardcover books. A best-selling book for under $5 is unheard of at Barnes & Noble, but it's usually the norm on Kindle.

And when customers are happy with a price point, they will keep buying. Amazon is known as the place where readers can find good books for an average of $4. And with *Kindle Unlimited*, they can access tens of thousands of books for a small monthly fee.

Since millions of readers are paying for these low-priced books, both Amazon and authors make money by the sheer volume of sales. Avid readers love Amazon Kindle books for this reason, hence why Amazon has the bulk share of eBook readers.

So how should you price your fiction Kindle eBooks? I recommend a price of $2.99 for your first book $2.99. I also recommend you enroll your first book in *Kindle Select,* even if it is for just 90 days. As a new author, you must do some work to bring in readers. A good cover and description are crucial for getting potential customers to even click on your book, much less download it.

You will want to study the competition in whatever category you publish in. See what other authors in your genre are charging for their books. You may find that in some troupes, almost all books are priced at 99 cents, with most of the profits coming from *Kindle Unlimited* subscribers, not people actually buying the books. On the other side, you may see some authors with a large following whose books aren't in *Kindle Select* and who are charging a bit more for their books.

After publishing for a while and having built up a following, you can reexamine your book pricing and whether or not you want your books enrolled in *Kindle Select.* However, note that it can take years to build up the level of readership that would allow you to charge more for your books and pull them from *Kindle Select.*

Pricing and royalties are different from fiction paperback books. For one thing, Amazon charges a printing fee for every book you sell on top of the 40% cut of the profits. Your 60% royalties come after the printing fee, hence why you have to price paperback books higher.

For indie authors on Amazon, most make the bulk of their money from Kindle eBooks. Now, that isn't to say that no one buys paperback books. Many customers will buy paperback books from authors they love. However, it usually takes a while to build a fan base of readers who will pay several dollars more for your paperback versus eBook.

Again, look at what other authors in your genre are pricing their paperback books at. Perhaps they sell their Kindle eBooks for $2.99 but have their paperback books priced at $9.99. With time, many established authors can raise prices for their Kindle and paperback books. But again, when you are just starting out, you want to make your books as affordable as possible.

Pricing for Non-Fiction Books: Non-fiction is the primary category I write in. While non-fiction books don't typically sell as well as fiction books do, the good part is that you can usually charge more for non-fiction books versus fiction books.

Non-fiction books range from cookbooks with full-color photos to textbooks filled with charts and graphs. And while many non-fiction books are published as eBooks, most successful non-fiction book authors make their money from selling paperback books.

For me, my eBook sales are about 10% of what my paperback sales are. At the time of this writing, none of my non-fiction books are enrolled in *Kindle Select*; and the sales of most of my books are paperbacks.

When I first started writing non-fiction, all of my books were available on Kindle only and were priced at $2.99. In 2020, I started publishing new versions of my best-selling books every year (an example is the book you are currently reading, which is the second year I've released a new version of this title). Not only did I start releasing new yearly versions, but I also started publishing my books in paperback.

I've mentioned before that publishing my books in paperback was the key to increasing my publishing income. Business books, in particular, do better in paperback than they do on Kindle. But to justify putting a book in paperback, it needs to be longer than the typical Kindle book.

Today I price most of my non-fiction Kindle books at $9.99, meaning I earn around $7 for each Kindle book I sell. I price most of my non-fiction paperback books at $16.99, meaning I earn around $7 for each paperback book I sell. $9.99 was the maximum I could charge for my Kindle books to earn the 70% royalty. And I wanted to earn the same amount of money whether a customer bought a Kindle or paperback book, hence why I chose $16.99 for my paperback books

Note that I have worked for years to build up my brand. I couldn't have sold my books for the prices I do now when I first started self-publishing. I had to work hard to prove to readers that I had written quality books that would teach them how to sell on Ebay, start a YouTube channel, and make money on Amazon KDP.

As with fiction, you want to see what other authors in your genre are charging for their non-fiction books. The more books available in a specific genre, the cheaper the prices may be as there is more competition.

A look at the Kindle non-fiction categories will give you the following list:

- Arts & Photography
- Biographies & Memoirs
- Business & Investing
- Children's Nonfiction

- Computers & Technology
- Cooking, Food & Wine
- Crafts, Hobbies & Home
- Education & Reference
- Engineering & Transportation
- Health, Fitness & Dieting
- History
- Law
- Literary Criticism & Theory
- Medical
- Parenting & Relationships
- Politics & Social Sciences
- Science
- Self-Help
- Sports
- Travel

Do some research within the category you are interested in writing in by digging through the best-sellers list. You will find a mix of both traditionally published and self-published titles.

For example, let's say you are interested in writing a cookbook. You will find thousands of cookbooks for sale for as low as 99 cents on Kindle to over $30 in hardcover. It's usually easy to notice the cookbooks by indie authors as they are the cheapest options and don't feature a celebrity chef on the cover.

Another trick is to look at the *Top 100 Free* lists within each category. These are books enrolled in *Kindle Select*, for which the authors currently offer free book promotions. Note that these free book offers are available for all Amazon customers, not just those with *Kindle Unlimited* memberships.

I like to look at the top-ranked free books and check out the author pages of those who wrote them. I look at how many books they have published and look at their revenue on *Publisher Rocket*. I also look at how they are pricing their books. Finally, I try to honestly look at how their books compare to mine. Are

ANN ECKHART

they shorter or longer? Do they have more reviews than my books? How does their revenue compare to mine?

That being said, I don't always follow the competition when it comes to pricing my books. My three top-selling books are usually ranked in the top 100 in the *Auctions & Small Business* category. There are other books in that category that are priced lower than mine, and that often rank higher. However, I choose to keep mine priced higher as I believe my books to be of higher quality. Plus, even if some of the Kindle versions are priced lower, I sell mostly paperbacks; and not all of the competition publish their books in paperback; they only offer Kindle books. Often the Kindle listing of my book leads people to my book's page, where they typically then buy the paperback copy.

Pricing Low-Content Books: No-and-low content books include journals, planners, notebooks, and activity books. I'll discuss these books in-depth in the last chapter of this book, but I will touch on their pricing here.

No-and-low content books have minimal or no content on the interior pages. Blank or lined notebooks, sketchbooks, or journals are defined at no content, as there is no text on the inside pages. Guided journals and activity books are considered low-content as there is some writing and/or images inside.

Pricing Notebooks: Notebooks are a dime a dozen on Amazon. Just like notebooks are inexpensive in stores, notebooks are inexpensive on Amazon, including those from major publishers such as Mead and Five Star.

One major downfall for self-publishing notebooks on Amazon is that they are not spiral-bound. Most people who purchase notebooks like them to be spiral-bound, but Amazon currently does not offer that option. Because you can't offer this feature, you need to focus on creating fun covers to entice shoppers to buy your notebooks.

Most notebooks are priced between $4.99 and $6.99 on Amazon.

It all depends on the size and page count, which affect the printing cost. We've discussed how Amazon takes out the printing price from the sale price of every paperback book. Your cut of the royalties on paperback books is 60% versus 70% for Kindle books.

People who make money selling notebooks are typically uploading thousands and thousands of designs, running a volume business. Most of my notebooks are 7x10-inch, which is composition notebook size, or 8.5x11, which is considered full-size. I also typically put 120 pages in my notebooks. Because they are larger than most notebooks on Amazon, I typically price mine at $6.99.

Pricing Journals: People self-publish both blank and guided journals on Amazon. Blank journals are typically 6x9 inches and feature around 100 pages. Therefore, they are priced on the low side of $3.99 to $4.99. At this low price, publishers barely make a dollar per sale. Just as people make money with tens of thousands of notebook designs, the same is true for a blank journal.

Guided journals are a higher quality product. Typically, each page of a guided journal includes a text prompt for users to fill out. I have a line of ancestry-guided journals filled with questions for users to answer about their life. Because guided journals have text and are a more complex product to create versus a blank journal, you can charge more for them.

There are 6x9-inch guided journals that are priced anywhere from $6.99 to $9.99, while larger sizes typically cost more. My ancestry-guided journals are 8.5x11-inch full-size books; therefore, I charge $14.95 for them. I also have 8x10-inch composition size guided journals for school-age children that I charge $11.95 for.

Planners: Planners sell extremely well on Amazon during the fourth quarter (October through December) as people buy them for themselves and as gifts. You can create a wide variety of planners (daily, weekly, monthly, yearly, or even undated) in all sizes (6x9-inch is the most popular size, but you can make them as big as 8.5x11-inch).

As with all paperback books, there is a printing cost involved that comes out of the sale price. The larger and thicker your planner is, the more it will cost to print. That means you will have to charge more to make a decent profit.

I personally like full-size 8.5x11-inch weekly planners. I include some custom pages in my planners, which make them thicker than usual. I typically sell these planners for $9.99, making around $3 on every sale after Amazon takes out the printing cost and their cut of the royalties.

Pricing Activity Books: Activity books, such as puzzle books and coloring books, have become a hot trend among self-publishers on Amazon. These types of books are highly sought after, but they also take more time and skill to create.

However, the competition is fierce because there are so many of these books for sale on Amazon, not just from self-publishers but also from traditional publishers. That means you can't price yours too high, or you will turn off potential customers.

I have several adult coloring books available on Amazon that I've priced at $7.99. I only make around $2 on each sale after Amazon takes out the printing costs and their share of the royalties.

TO RECAP: Pricing your self-published books on Amazon is something that you will likely change frequently as you learn what customers are willing to pay as well as what your competition is doing. Just like there are many things you can update in your listings, even after you have hit publish, you can change the pricing of your books at any time.

CHAPTER TEN: HOW TO ADVERTISE & MARKET YOUR BOOKS

You've done it! Your book has been researched, written, edited, and uploaded with an eye-catching cover. Now that your book is available for sale on Amazon, you can just kick back and watch the money roll in, right? Wrong! Getting your book published is just the beginning. Now the work of getting people to buy it begins!

Self-publishing means that you write, edit, upload, and promote your book yourself. There is no agent or publishing house behind you; if you want people to find your book and buy it, it is up to you to get the word out. Self-published authors are not just writers and editors but also their own advertising agencies. I spend just as much time marketing my books as I do writing them.

But how do you spread the word about your book to generate sales? To start, you will need to utilize social media. Facebook, Twitter, Pinterest, Instagram, YouTube, and TikTok can all be used to drive traffic to your books on Amazon effectively.

The great thing about social media is that it is easy and free. The chances are that you already use these sites yourself, so learning how to utilize them to market your books is relatively simple, albeit somewhat time-consuming. However, you do not have to use every single site if you do not want to; certain genres do better on specific sites. Some authors only use one or two, while others use them all. What you choose to do is up to you.

Facebook: Part of promoting yourself as an author is "branding" yourself as one, and a social media presence is the easiest way to accomplish this. Creating a **Facebook page for your author business** offers more ways for you to connect with your readers than Twitter, Pinterest, and Instagram combined.

A Facebook business page differs from a personal one, although you must first have a personal Facebook account to set up a business page. A personal Facebook page is one where people *friend* you, while a business page is one people *like*.

A personal Facebook page limits your number of friends, but you can have limitless *likes* on your business page. Both people and products can have Facebook business pages. You likely already *like* or *follow* several celebrities and business Facebook pages.

While it can take a while to build up the number of *likes* on a Facebook business page, I still believe it is important to set one up separately from your personal Facebook page. I have seen many people, both authors and other small business owners, start with a personal Facebook page that they made public to followers, only to eventually reach the maximum number of *friends* allowed. They then had to scramble to create a Facebook business page and encourage people to *like* that page.

Facebook users are more accustomed to *friending* people than *liking* pages, so it usually takes longer to build a business page than a friend list, making it tempting to have a friend page. But if you want your readership following to grow, starting a business page for your author's name is best. Plus, you always want to keep your personal life and business separate; if you use pen names, you may not even want your friends and family to know that you are writing books!

Because I already had an established Facebook page before I started writing books, it was easy for me to start promoting my non-fiction books via my social networking sites, including Facebook. However, if you have a Facebook page for your plumbing business, it will not be a good fit to promote your romance novels! I have my main business page for my non-fiction books, YouTube videos, and affiliate marketing, but I now have three other business pages, one for my print-on-demand books and one for each of my fiction pen names.

To set up a Facebook business page for your publishing business, visit: facebook.com/pages/creation.

You can create a separate Facebook page for each of your pen names, if applicable. Facebook makes it easy to toggle back and forth between your personal account and business page. Just go to your profile picture in the top right-hand corner of Facebook to switch between pages.

I use Facebook pages in different ways to promote my books. My main Facebook page, @anneckhart, is where I promote everything I do under my own name, including my non-fiction books. I also promote my YouTube videos there. And I will cross-post my Etsy sticker shop and low-content books, which have their own page @jeanleepublishing, on my main Facebook page, too.

I utilize my fiction Facebook pages differently. There is no cross-promotion between my main page, my Etsy shop, and my low-content books with my fiction pen names. Most people who follow my @anneckhart page and my @jeanleepublishing page have no idea I have fiction books published under different pen names. And I prefer to keep it that way.

On my fiction Facebook pages, I share when I release new books and when I run any specials, such as free book promotions. I sometimes ask questions of my followers to create engagement; this could be a book-related question (such as what their favorite books are or what types of stories they enjoy reading) or just something fun (such as asking what their favorite foods or activities are) to get my follows to "like" or comment on posts.

With my fiction readers, I feel it's more important to create engagement directly with the people buying my fiction books. With my non-fiction and low-content books, I can take a more direct selling approach. People who read fiction books like to discuss plots and characters. People who buy non-fiction books usually just want to get the information they paid for and move on. Still, followers will still "like" the posts on my non-fiction and low-content pages, even if they don't comment the way fiction readers do.

Encouraging any type of engagement with your followers, whether through likes or comments, is essential in keeping your page active and gaining new followers. Facebook has made it increasingly difficult for people to see business posts, suppressing or even outright hiding posts from business pages, as they want those of us with business pages to pay for the posts to be seen. Therefore, it is important to do more than just post links to your books to engage your audience. Even adding a few emojis can go a long way towards catching your followers' eyes and causing them to pause and engage with your post and perhaps even click on your link.

One of the best ways to create engagement is to add in posts that don't have direct links to your products. The rule of thumb is to post one business post and then three general posts to keep followers engaged. While it's tempting to just post links to your books, breaking up your business posts with other fun posts shows your followers you aren't just trying to sell them something but also engage with them.

An easy way to create engagement outside of links to your books is to post funny memes or photos. You want to keep this type of content clean as you hope to appeal to a broad audience. But these types of posts always create a lot of engagement for me. I do not just post book-related memes but also general ones. You can find memes posted all over the internet. To find book-themed memes, simply do a Google search. You will be presented with all types of funny graphics that are easy to share on your page.

Your posts and photos do not always have to relate to your business, either; you want to develop a personal relationship with your readers by sharing other aspects of your life. For instance, my Facebook followers love when I post pictures of my dogs and my elderly father (they know him as "Papa").

Of course, if you are using a pen name that you want to keep private, you need to be careful about posting anything that would lead followers to your real name. This can be difficult as it is common practice for authors to post their own headshot as their profile picture. I get around this by using a graphic of my pen name as my author photo. But it is something to consider as you embark on your self-publishing journey.

Another advantage of getting your followers to "like" and comment on your posts is that sometimes this activity will show up on a person's Facebook feed for their friends and family to see, which may encourage others to follow you, too. You have likely seen this happen on your own Facebook feed, where it will show you that a friend liked a post or a page. The convenient "like" thumbs-up icon will be there, making it easy for you, too, to "like" the page.

It is always my hope that when someone "likes" one of my posts that their friends will see it, check out my page, and then "like" it, too. As I mentioned earlier, Facebook shows status updates and photos more than links; so I get more "likes" and comments on my status updates and photos than I do when I simply post links to my books.

However, do not neglect to promote your books. A good rule of thumb is one business post for every three personal/fun posts. That way, your followers will not feel that you are only connecting with them in a push to sell them something.

As your readership grows, you will likely find that people want to "friend" you on your personal Facebook page. Even if you are not promoting your personal page, it will still be easy for most people to find, especially if your business page is your author's name, which is likely what your personal page is named, too.

Unless it is a reader you have gotten to know well, I strongly encourage you NOT to add readers as friends on Facebook. You want to maintain some privacy with a division between your personal and public/business life. While many of my friends and family do "like" my Facebook business pages, not all do. And none of them even know my fiction pen names, as I kept those a secret.

I use my Facebook business page to promote my books and YouTube videos and save my personal information for my personal Facebook account. While it can be hard to turn down friend requests from well-meaning people, I only accept Facebook "friend" requests from my actual friends and family for safety and security reasons. Readers need to "like" my Facebook business page to connect with me.

I have also set up my personal Facebook page with the tightest security settings to protect myself, and I have turned off the private messaging settings on my business pages so that people cannot send me direct messages. I did this because I found myself inundated with long messages from people wanting advice on writing books or just someone to chat with. While most of these messages were harmless, it took a lot of my time and energy to deal with all the questions.

Again, just as it is hard to deny friend requests, it can be hard to ignore messages. However, that is when I reminded myself that my books are my business. I must protect myself and my family by guarding my personal information as much as possible. And I need to make the best use of my work hours by writing and promoting my books, not dealing with messages.

Facebook Advertising: Facebook also offers advertising options, which can be a great way to sell books. Once you have a business page and start posting on it, you will see that Facebook offers you the option to "boost" your post. "Boosting" is just creating an advertisement. Facebook offers you two ways to advertise:

1. **"Boosting" posts**, meaning when you post a status update or link, you can pay to have Facebook show the post to an audience you choose. OR
2. **Facebook Ads**, where you create a specific ad and pay for Facebook to show it to an audience you choose.

I have used both models effectively. I like to use the "boost" option to promote my YouTube videos and special book promotions, such as if I am running a free book offer. For these types of "boosts," I typically choose for Facebook to push them out to the people who follow my page and their friends and family. This is a good way for my regular followers not only to see the post but their Facebook friends and family will be shown the post and shows that they are friends with someone who likes my page. This tactic not only helps me promote my video or book but also helps me gain more followers on my respective pages.

The "boost" option will appear under your posts. You will need to set up a **Facebook advertising account** first so that Facebook can charge you for your ads. Facebook will prompt you to do this the first time you attempt to "boost" a post or create an ad.

There are two ways to access the Facebook Advertising page: either from your personal page (look for the **Ad Manager** link on the left-hand side of your feed) or directly on your business page (look for the **Ad Center** link on the left-hand side of your business page feed). You will also likely have a **Promote** button at the top of your page. All three of these links will take you to the same page where you can create Facebook ads.

Running ads to a website (in this case, your Amazon Author Page) differs from local businesses advertising to local customers. Facebook offers Automated Ad features, but I have found this to work best for local brick-and-mortar businesses as Facebook uses local data to drive traffic to those ads.

To advertise books, I click on the **Create New Ad** option, which allows me to make an ad using text, photos, or videos and to select my own audience. A new page will open with Create Ad at the top.

When I am running a Facebook ad for one of my books, my main goal is to get people over to my Amazon Author Page or to the individual page for a particular book. Therefore, I select the **Get more website visitors** option under **Goals**.

Next up is the **Ad Creative.** Here is where you can really get creative by designing unique ads, either creating them yourself or hiring a graphic designer to make them. Since I typically run ads to only one book, I usually just enter the link to the book and let the ad be the book's image from Amazon, which will insert automatically.

There is an entire industry around creating effective Facebook book ads. Just as you can hire proofreaders and book cover artists on websites such as Fiverr.com and UpWork.com, you can also hire designers to create Facebook ads for you. However, when starting out, it is perfectly fine to use your book's cover as it appears on Amazon.

Under *Ad Creative,* you will need to write a **Description**. Amazon will likely pre-fill in some text for you, but this is where you want to really sell your book so that people who see your ad will click on it. If I was writing ad copy for an Ebay book, I might put in something like, "Looking to start your own business? Learn how to make money online from home by selling on Ebay!"

Some fiction authors will put the first few paragraphs of their book, or a particularly sensational section of their book, in the *Description*, hoping it will draw readers in. It is a good idea to experiment with different ad text to find the best style for the types of books you write.

Under **Audience** is where you will select to who Facebook shows your ad to. You can select **Smart Audience** and let Facebook decide where to place your ad, but I strongly prefer to choose my audience myself. For my fiction books, I will choose to have my ads target authors in my genre, hoping that fans of specific authors may also be interested in my books.

However, finding these targeted authors can be very difficult as the author needs to have a large enough following on Facebook for you to be able to select them as a target. Most self-published authors do not show up in Facebook's targeting list, so you will have to figure out which of the big-name authors to target.

You may think you would want to target the biggest names in publishing regardless, but self-published authors heavily populate the Amazon fiction market. And while these writers may not be on Facebook's radar, they are on Amazon's. So, finding authors in Facebook's system can be challenging.

You can also target your ads to people who like specific topics or activities. And you will need to choose the location, age range, and gender of Facebook users you want your ads shown to. For instance, if you are writing historical romance, your audience will likely be women over thirty. That is different from writing a young adult thriller where your audience might be college-age men. Figuring out who your audience is is crucial when it comes to Facebook ads.

Finally, you will need to choose the **Duration** your ad will run and the **Daily Budget**. I recommend starting with an ad that will run continuously rather than selecting an end date. Don't worry; you can pause or end your ads anytime.

As for your daily budget, I recommend starting with $5 per day. If the ad proves successful, you can always increase your budget. You pay for your ads via the clicks they receive. The more clicks, the faster your ad budget will be eaten up.

So how will you know if an ad is successful? After all, people may click on your ad, for which Facebook will charge you; but neither Facebook nor Amazon will tell you if someone purchased your book from a Facebook ad.

To determine if a Facebook ad is working, you must rely on monitoring your book's rank. If you are getting Facebook ad clicks and also seeing your book's rank rise, it is likely to result from the ad. You can test this by turning the ad off for a period and seeing if your rank drops. If it does, you can assume that your Facebook ad was working and can turn it back on.

Facebook Groups: Another valuable Facebook tool that fiction writers, in particular, use is **Facebook Groups**. Facebook allows business pages to create private groups, and this type of group is hugely popular in the fiction author community.

I have a Facebook group for my fiction pen name (my fiction readers know both of my pen names, so I promote both pen names within one group), but not for my non-fiction books. However, I have a Facebook group that I started for my Etsy sticker shop, which shares the same name as my low-content books. While I mainly use the group to share my stickers and magnets with customers, when I have a new low-content book available, I will also post it there.

A handy feature of Facebook is that you can connect your Facebook group to its corresponding Facebook page. For instance, my sticker group is linked directly to my @jeanleepublishing page. When I post something to my @jeanleepublishing page, a pop-up window appears asking if I also want to share the post with my sticker group. It's a quick and easy way to share the post to both my business page and my private group.

With fiction especially, authors want to create a community of their readers; there is no easier way to do that than by creating a private Facebook group exclusively for readers. You can promote your group with a link in the back of your books, on your Facebook page, and on your other social media sites. You can then engage with your readers directly by answering questions, hosting giveaways, and sharing updates about your forthcoming books.

A Facebook group is also the best place to find BETA readers for your books. I will discuss BETA readers later in this chapter.

Twitter: Like Facebook, Twitter provides a free and easy way to connect with readers and drive traffic to your books. Amazon makes it super easy to "tweet" out direct links to your book by using the little Twitter icon located on your book's page.

Twitter allows you 280 characters in each Tweet, so you have plenty of room for text, a link to your book, and **hashtags**. *Hashtags* are simply keywords that follow a pound (#) sign. For instance, when I Tweet out the link to my book, *101 Items To Sell On Ebay*, I add hashtags such as #Ebay, #thrifting, #reselling, #picking, #makingmoneyonline, and/or #workfromhome.

Savvy Twitter users search for Tweets using *hashtags*, so adding them to your Twitter posts is another way to drive traffic to your books. I have noticed a significant increase in my book sales since I started using *hashtags*. You can also use *hashtags* such as #author and #writer if you want to find other self-published authors to connect with.

I set aside a few minutes every evening to connect with other Twitter users, which I can do easily on my iPhone while relaxing in front of the TV. I retweet posts I like, reply to others, and post a Tweet or two of my own. Twitter works best when you actively engage with other users, so spending a few minutes each day working on Twitter to grow your followers is important.

Note that Twitter is not as popular as it once was, so do not be discouraged if you have a slow time gaining followers. Keep sharing content, interact with other users, and allow your following to grow naturally. Twitter accounts can also end up in Google searches, so it is important to have an active account to increase the chance of people finding you even when they are not on Twitter's site.

Pinterest: Pinterest is often overlooked when it comes to promoting books, but, as with Facebook and Twitter, it is another free and easy way to drive traffic to your titles.

I have several boards on Pinterest, including several for my businesses. I have created the following boards for pinning my business content:

- Home-based business board (for my Ebay, YouTube, and Amazon KDP books and planners)
- Notebooks, planners, and journals board (for my low-content books)
- Adult coloring books board (for the coloring books I have for sale on Amazon)
- Stickers board (for my Etsy shop)
- Magnets board (for my Etsy shop)
- YouTube board (for my YouTube videos)

As you post to Pinterest, you may find yourself invited to join groups with similar interests, both for readers and authors. This is another great way for more people to find your "pins" and hopefully click through to your books. Pinterest works best when you interact with other users, so re-pinning their pins is another way to get yourself, your pins, and your books noticed.

Instagram: Instagram offers another free, easy, and fun way to interact with your readers and to gain new followers for your publishing business. Instagram allows you to share photos and short videos and "like" and comment on content shared by others.

As with Facebook, I have separate Instagram accounts for my business books, my low-content books/Etsy shop Instagram, and for each of my fiction pen names. Instagram makes it easy to create multiple accounts under one main user account, and switching back and forth between them is as simple as tapping on your screen name.

If you create an Instagram account for your books, whether under your own name or a pen name, make sure that the link in your Instagram profile is your Amazon Author Page to make it easy for followers to click through to your library. You want an active, clickable link that people can quickly follow.

When promoting my books on Instagram, I simply download a copy of the cover directly from Amazon (you can right-click-save or take a screenshot) and post it to both my main feed and to my stories. I always make sure to add "link in bio" to all my posts. If you post to your "stories," you can add a direct link that people can click on, which will take them directly to your book's listing on Amazon.

The best use of Instagram I have found is to connect with readers on a more personal level. I share photos of my dogs and family on Instagram. I will also share pictures of fun activities, such as eating dinner out at a restaurant or attending local events. I also post funny memes, which always create a lot of engagement. Whatever the photo content, however, the main goal is to further connect with followers who are interested in the content I am providing, including the books I write.

I also utilize *hashtags* on Instagram. As with Twitter, *hashtags* are a smart way for Instagram users to find posts. While not all these users will become Instagram followers, they may just click through to your books, resulting in more potential buyers for your books. You can also connect with other authors on Instagram with the *hashtags* #writersofinstagram and #authorsofinstagram.

YouTube: One of the best ways I have been able to promote my books is through my YouTube channels. I currently have two: a vlog channel and a channel devoted to sit-down videos. While my books are not the main topic of my videos, I do talk about them on camera. And the first link under all my videos leads viewers to my Amazon Author Page.

There is an active self-publishing community on YouTube, from authors to marketers and avid readers. Take the time to seek out other authors in your genre as well as readers who may be interested in your books to see what types of videos they are creating. While making YouTube videos does take more time and effort, it can be a valuable tool in your book marketing kit.

LinkedIn: LinkedIn is a social media site for professionals. It is used more like a resume website and networking tool than it is for promotion. However, it is free and easy to set up an account there, so there is no harm in creating your profile.

TikTok: The newest social media website is TikTok, which specializes in short videos. It initially gained popularity with young people creating dances to popular songs, but it has exploded to appeal to all ages and demographics, including authors and readers. #authortok and #booktok are just two of the popular *hashtags* the publishing community uses on TikTok.

If you are a fiction writer, a popular video format is to read a short summary of your book as one of your characters, especially one that ends in a question. Something like, "My husband left me for another woman, but now he wants me back. What should I do?" The answer is, of course, to find out by reading the book!

Many authors on TikTok communicate with their fans by answering reader questions or simply sharing some of their personal lives. As with all social media, you want to ensure your Amazon Author Page is in your TikTok profile so followers can go directly to your books. You can also link Instagram and YouTube accounts to TikTok.

Note that Instagram and TikTok only allow one link in your bio. This is frustrating when, like me, you may have numerous links. I have an Amazon author page, an Amazon store, an Etsy shop, an Ebay store, two YouTube channels, and several other social media accounts. I need more than just one link.

Fortunately, there are sites such as **linktr.ee** where you can create a landing page with all your links that are accessible with just one link. My linktr.ee is **linktr.ee/anneckhart.** When you click on my linktr.ee link on Instagram or TikTok, it opens up a new window with all of my links. There are paid linktr.ee options with extra features, but the free version works well for most people.

A good plan for TikTok when you are starting is to post three times a day. Make one post about your books and make the other two something lighthearted and funny. Post the book content in the evening when more people are on the app. As with other posts on social media, you want to break up the "selling" posts with more general content to attract more followers and not make people feel as if you are always trying to sell them something.

Blog/Website: For years, I maintained a blog and promoted my books on it. But in 2020, I shut it down, deciding that my other social media sites worked just fine to market my non-fiction books. I do not have a website for my print-on-demand books, either; relying on social media to promote those products, too.

However, I do have a dedicated website for my fiction pen name. While I do the bulk of the marketing of my fiction books on social media and on Amazon itself, a website allows me to have a place where people can sign up for my mailing list. And in the fiction world, a mailing list is everything. I will discuss mailing lists more later in this chapter.

You can create a website on sites such as GoDaddy.com and Wix.com. Both provide easy options for setting up a basic site. You want your library of books on your site with links to them on Amazon. You also want to have your social media sites linked and a way for people to contact you.

Even if you don't want a blog or website, consider securing your personalized URL web addresses from a site such as GoDaddy.com. I own the URL anneckhart.com and have it pointed to my Amazon Author page.

While having a dedicated website can be a good idea, I believe it should be the last thing you set up as you begin your self-publishing journey. Work on your social media sites first before worrying about a website.

Networking: It is not enough to just share the link to your book with potential customers. You must engage not only readers but other authors. Look for writing groups on Facebook. Follow all the self-published author accounts on Twitter. Offer tips on reading and perhaps reviewing books from other authors on your Instagram, TikTok, or YouTube channel. Establishing yourself as an author, writer, reader, and businessperson goes hand in hand when it comes to selling books. And that means networking with authors, marketers, and customers.

Free Book Promotions: If you signed up for KDP Select, you could offer your Kindle eBooks for free for up to five days per every 90-day enrollment period. However, these free book promotions have definite pros and cons.

The pros of free book promotions are getting your book into the hands of Amazon readers. When you are just starting with your first book, you have no name recognition, following, or readers waiting to read what you have written. So, one way to get people to read your book is to give it to them for free.

If enough people download your free book, the book will climb up the ranks of Amazon's free best-sellers lists. Yes, Amazon has best-seller lists for books people buy and for books people get for free. Being on any of Amazon's best-seller lists will help you be seen by more potential readers, which will be especially helpful the more books you publish.

Offering your book for free is also a way to get reviews for it, hopefully. However, this is where the biggest con in free book promotions lies: people who get the free books are often the ones who can leave the worst reviews.

I have had two instances where I have released a book, offered it for free, and immediately received one-star negative reviews. Now, no matter how good a book might be, someone somewhere will eventually leave a bad review. A few bad reviews over the years are to be expected.

But when the negative review is the first and only review for a book? Let me just say that I may have sat in my car at the bank crying for an hour when this happened to me. It was devasting to check my phone and see that someone had ripped my book to shreds.

Fortunately, other reviews soon came in, burying those negative reviews. However, it was a very upsetting time as I feared one bad review would destroy my hard work. I tried to take solace in the fact both people who left me those negative reviews had histories of leaving bad reviews for every book they read (you can see the review history of anyone who posts a review on Amazon).

However, in both instances, the first reviews of these books were awful, which meant my newly released books sat on Amazon's website with sad little one-star ratings for a couple of days until more reviews came through. I could tell from the rankings and sales reports that those reviews hurt the launches of both of those books. And reviews are what help sell books.

There is a way to ensure that your book has good reviews when it is released, and that is with BETA readers.

BETA Readers: How can you ensure that your book launches with positive reviews? BETA readers! BETA readers receive an advanced copy of your book. In exchange for the free book, BETA readers will proofread your work, catching any last-minute errors; they agree to leave your book a review the day it goes live.

How do you find BETA readers? Remember those Facebook groups I talked about earlier in this chapter? Most authors get their BETA readers from those groups. When I have finished writing a book, I post to my Facebook group asking for BETA readers. I tell them they will get a free copy of the book (a computer file, not a physical book) in exchange for them proofreading it and then leaving a review when it launches.

Many authors, including me, use **BookFunnel.com** to send out these advance reader copies to BETA readers. Plans start at only $20 a year, making it an easy and affordable way to send your book to BETA readers. BookFunnel sends them your book's file and will even send them reminders when their corrections are due and when to leave their reviews.

But how do you get people to join your Facebook group so that you can have BETA readers? How do you reach potential readers before your book is even published? The answer is a mailing list.

Mailing List: In the fiction world, a mailing list is the ultimate publishing tool. Creating and building an email database of fans who will buy every book you publish separates the successful authors from those who struggle to sell even one copy of their book. A mailing list can provide you with people who will join your private Facebook group and would also love to be one of your BETA readers.

But how do you build a mailing list when you haven't yet published a book?

BEGINNER'S GUIDE TO AMAZON KDP: 2023 EDITION

Before you can build a mailing list, you need to have a mailing list provider. Since I started my author website early on, I have used the email subscription service included with my website package. However, there are numerous websites you can use to build your mailing list, including:

- AuthorEmail.com
- ConstantContact.com
- ConvertKit.com
- MailerLite.com
- MailChimp.com

Prices and features vary among these websites, but all will allow you to collect email addresses and send out mass email campaigns. But you need to entice people to sign up for your mailing list, and you do that with a Reader Magnet.

A reader magnet is a freebie given to someone in return for them giving you their email address. In the self-publishing world, that freebie is usually a short story or the first chapter of a book. Some authors even give out entire novels for free. If you write non-fiction, your reader magnet might be a how-to guide or tutorial. Whatever your reader magnet is, users must subscribe to your email list to get it.

I mentioned BookFunnel earlier as the best way to send advance book copies to BETA readers, and it can also serve as a website to handle your reader magnets. You can load your reader magnet onto BookFunnel and provide a link to potential mailing list subscribers via your social media accounts. For instance, once your reader magnet is ready, you can post the link to Facebook, boosting the post to reach more potential readers. People love freebies, so it is usually not too difficult to start getting people to sign up.

BookFunnel provides several options for book magnets, including collecting the email addresses of those who take advantage of your offer, which you can then integrate into your mailing list provider. You can set up an automated "welcome" message for anyone who signs up for your reader magnet that invites them to join your Facebook group.

To Recap: I realize that I just gave you a lot of information and that you may feel overwhelmed. After all, you probably just want to write a book and get it published. But to make money in self-publishing, you must also market and promote it. Advertising is key to selling self-published books.

Here is a step-by-step list to follow that will help keep you on track:

1. Secure your personalized URL on a site such as GoDaddy.com
2. Create a Facebook page for your pen name, even if it is your legal name
3. Create a reader group on Facebook
4. Create a Twitter account specifically for your author name
5. Create an Instagram account for your author name
6. Consider creating a TikTok account and YouTube account for your author name. You don't have to utilize either, at least not immediately, but lock in the names as soon as possible.
7. Create a linktr.ee account with all of your links included
8. Sign up with BookFunnel.com
9. Sign up with an email list service
10. Create your reader magnet and load it onto BookFunnel
11. Promote your reader magnet on social media
12. Create a mailing list from the emails gained from the reader magnet
13. Invite those who signed up to your mailing list to join your Facebook group
14. Invite those in your Facebook group to be BETA readers

15. Send out advanced copies of your book to your BETA readers via BookFunnel.com

Friends & Family: I bet you have wondered why I have not mentioned getting friends and family to review your books. I mean, certainly, they would leave you glowing reviews, right? Well, there is a reason I left this section for last, and that is because you need to be very careful about having people in your personal life leave your Amazon book reviews. Here is why:

Amazon does not allow you to pay for reviews. I mentioned earlier in this book about Amazon suing Fiverr accounts for selling paid reviews. Amazon was able to track down these reviewing services and had them shut down.

If you have sent a friend or family member a gift or gift card through Amazon and then that person leaves you a book review without having a record of buying the book, Amazon may assume that you paid for their review. And if you are flagged as paying for book reviews, Amazon could shut down your account. And when Amazon bans you, it is nearly impossible to get back on their site.

So, it will not matter if you did not pay your mom to review your book; if you sent her something through Amazon and Amazon connects her account to yours in any way, they will first likely delete the review. But if other people connected to your account keep trying to leave reviews, it can result in your account being banned. I would rather have an awkward conversation with my family and friends about not leaving reviews for my books than have to deal with Amazon possibly cracking down on my account.

How Amazon Will Know: We've covered that you don't want to pay for book reviews. And you don't want your friends and family to leave reviews. Instead, you want to have BETA readers leave you reviews. But how are BETA reader reviews different from paid reviews? And how will Amazon differentiate BETA readers from family and friends?

First, Amazon can figure out accounts that are being paid to leave reviews because they are leaving hundreds of reviews. It's one thing to log onto Amazon and leave a couple of reviews for products you've recently ordered. It's another to suddenly see one account loading a considerable number of reviews at once. Many of these paid services use software to leave mass reviews. Amazon, however, is now easily able to see this. This is what led to Fiverr sellers being sued for selling review services.

Second, remember that for your friends and family, the issue comes from their accounts being linked to yours in the form of your addresses being entered and used for sending each other gifts. I have sent most of my extended family and close friends gift cards from Amazon at one time or another. So if they were to log into Amazon and leave me a book review, Amazon's system would see the link. But as long as you haven't sent a BETA reader something from your Amazon account, you are safe from Amazon thinking you sent a gift to someone in exchange for a review. This is a good thing to remember if you decide to do giveaways. Make sure any prizes you mail out to your BETA readers are not sent from Amazon but directly from you.

Amazon understands that authors use BETA readers for book launches and reviews. They are okay with the process of using BETA readers who don't purchase your book but leave a review for it. After all, people leave Amazon product reviews for items they didn't purchase but received as gifts. The issue is having a link between your account and that of someone who leaves you a review. Make sure there is no link, and you'll be fine.

TO RECAP: When you are a self-published author, all of your marketing and advertising falls on your shoulders. As you gain success, you may be able to hire these jobs out. However, when you are just starting out, you want to work these resources, most of which are free to use, as much as possible.

Make a daily checklist to complete your postings on your various social media pages. Keep things fun and lighthearted but also stay professional. Be sure to engage with your followers by replying to comments. Remember that it takes time to build a following and gain readers. But if you are consistent, the followers, the readers, and eventually, the money will come!

CHAPTER ELEVEN:
AMAZON ADS
FOR AUTHORS

Some books sell well organically on Amazon. Whether it is because the topic is in a relatively small genre with little competition or because readers have latched onto it, there are self-published authors who do very little, if any, paid marketing for their books.

Then there are the rest of us! The book market is crowded enough from the big-name publishing houses. Add when competing with tens of thousands of self-published authors, getting your book noticed by Amazon customers can feel nearly impossible.

Fortunately, there is one tool that Amazon offers to help you get your books noticed, and that is **Amazon Advertising**.

With *Amazon Advertising,* you can run advertisements for your books directly on Amazon's website, right in front of customers who are already searching for books to buy. Now, I know you might scoff at the idea of having to pay for your books to be seen on the very same website where they are published, but remember that you are competing with hundreds of thousands of other books. And unless you publish a best-seller right out of the gate, chances are you will need to at least try *Amazon Advertising* to generate borrows from any books enrolled in *Kindle Select* as well as sales of your paperback books.

According to Amazon's data, 30% of readers commonly browse Amazon for books, which is 30% of *global* visitors to Amazon's website. Also, 65% of readers discover new books while shopping on Amazon. There is a ready and willing market for books, and ads give you a chance to reach buyers who are already searching through the book categories.

How effective are Amazon ads when it comes to selling books? According to Amazon:

- 76% of global surveyed book buyers who research a book on Amazon recall seeing an ad for the book on the site
- 62% of global surveyed book buyers who discover a title or author while shopping on Amazon go on to purchase that title or other books by that author, either on Amazon or elsewhere
- 55% of global surveyed book buyers who visited Amazon say Amazon provided information that made them feel confident in their purchase, a statistic that continues to make Amazon the number one bookseller

Amazon offers three unique methods for advertising books:

Sponsored Products: Cost-per-click (CPC) ads that promote individual product listings on Amazon are referred to as **Sponsored Product Ads**. *Sponsored Product Ads* appear right where customers will see them on Amazon, such as on the first page of shopping results and on product pages of individual listings. You set the amount of money you are willing to spend per click, and you only pay when a customer clicks on your ad. Setting a daily budget allows you to control costs

Sponsored Brands: Cost-per-click (CPC) ads that feature your brand logo, a brief headline, and multiple products that appear at the top and bottom of search results. This is an excellent option if you have several similar books, such as a series. These ads appear in relevant shopping results and help drive the discovery of your brand among customers who are shopping for similar items on Amazon's website. As with *Sponsored Product Ads*, you only pay when a customer clicks on an ad; and you set both the per-click price and the daily budget.

Lockscreen Ads: Lockscreen Ads are exclusive to publishers in the United States. These ads appear on Amazon devices such as Kindle readers and Fire tablets, making your book front and center on the screen before users open their devices. However, these ads are more expensive than *Sponsored Product* and *Sponsored Brand* ads, making them more helpful to authors who already have a large following.

Most self-published authors focus on *Sponsored Product Ads* and *Sponsored Brand Ads*. *Lockscreen Ads* are typically used for successful, established authors.

Sponsored Product Ads and *Sponsored Brand Ads* are the two options I use myself. Both are relatively easy to learn and manage; and, done right, can increase your book's sales.

To start with Amazon Advertising, you first need to create an account at advertising.amazon.com. It is free and easy to create an account. Because you will be paying for ads, you will need to provide Amazon with a payment method where they can charge you for your advertising, meaning you will need to supply either a debit or credit card. You can also supply a bank account to have the funds withdrawn directly.

Once your account is active, you can set up your first ad. In the *Amazon Advertising* dashboard, there is a blue **Create campaign** button about halfway down the page. Click on this button to open up a new page titled **Choose your campaign type.**

Here you will choose from *Sponsored Products, Sponsored Brands,* or *Lockscreen Ads.* Let's start with **Sponsored Products,** which is the default option, by clicking on the **Continue** icon, which will bring up the **Create campaign** screen.

The first section is **Ad Format.** Here you will choose whether you want a:

- **Custom text ad:** You can add custom text to your ad to give customers a glimpse of your book. Think of it as adding a sentence or two to entice customers to click on your book ad; OR
- **Standard ad:** This creates an ad without custom text, one that shows your book cover, star rating, and price only.

Both options work equally well for non-fiction, as your covers should convey what your book is about. However, creating a *Custom text ad* can be beneficial for fiction books since there is so much competition. I tend to stick to *Standard ads* for my non-fiction and low-content books as I do not have to worry about writing ad copy. For this example, which is an Ebay book, we will choose *Standard ad.*

The next section is **Products.** Here is where you will choose the book or books you want to advertise. The reason I say "books" is that I often create ads using both the Kindle and paperback versions of a book. So, for my book, *Beginner's Guide To Selling On Ebay,* I will add both the Kindle version and the paperback version to my products list. I will not, however, add in my other Ebay books; I will create separate ads for separate book titles.

Next, you will choose the **Targeting,** either **Automatic Targeting** or **Manual Targeting.** If you are entirely new to self-publishing, you might want to try the *Automatic Targeting* option, allowing Amazon to use targeted keywords and products like the product in your ad.

For instance, if you are advertising a romance novel, Amazon will try to match your book to others on the market. However, once you have gained experience creating ads, you will likely want to use *Manual Targeting,* which allows you to select the keywords or products you want your ad to appear next to.

If you choose *Automatic Targeting*, you will then move onto the next section where you would select your default bid. Amazon will give you a high bid price, but you always want to start low. If the ad isn't being delivered, you can raise your bid later.

If you choose *Manual Targeting*, you will move onto the next section and choose **Keyword targeting** or **Product targeting.**

Keyword Targeting lets you select specific keywords and short phrases that customers typically search for on Amazon. You can create your own list, use the keywords Amazon suggests, or use a combination of both. You can also invest in keyword-generating software such as **Publisher Rocket**, which you can purchase at **publisherrocket.com.** I'll be discussing Publisher Rocket more later on in this chapter.

Product targeting lets you choose specific products, categories, or brands to directly target your ad to. You can use *Publisher Rocket* to find competitor products and additional categories your book may fall under. I like to target categories, myself.

Most people start off with keyword ads, so for this example, we will use *Keyword targeting.*

For example, let's say I am creating a *Keyword Targeting* ad for one of my Ebay books. As soon as I select the book I want to advertise, and Amazon will generate a long list of keywords related to that book. For my Ebay books, it typically suggests things like Ebay, Ebay business, *home-based business, how to sell on Ebay, selling Ebay, Ebay what sell,* and dozens more words and phrases.

You can see that the keywords are often two or three words together because this is what Amazon customers are typing into the search bar. A customer who comes to Amazon searching for a book about Ebay typically is not typing in, "I am looking for a book about how to sell things on Ebay." They are choosing a short phrase instead, including just the word *Ebay*.

In addition, once a customer begins typing words into the Amazon search bar, Amazon will start auto-filling suggestions for them. When I type *Ebay* into the Amazon search bar, several options appear that I could select, such as *Ebay gift card, ebay.com*, and *Ebay tape*.

You may be thinking that, of course, I would not want keywords such as *Ebay tape* in the ad for my Ebay book, but the fact that Amazon is suggesting that keyword to me shows that people are actively buying Ebay tape on Amazon. And if they are buying Ebay tape, maybe they would also be interested in an Ebay book. Hence why *Ebay tape* is a good keyword for my ad.

Back on the *Amazon Advertising* page and in the *Keyword targeting* section, you have a few decisions to make. The first is if you will use the **Suggested** keywords Amazon provides, if you will **Enter list**, or if you will **Upload a file** (a keyword list that you have saved in CSV, TSV, or XLSX). Uploading files is for advanced users, so we will stick to *Suggested* and *Enter list.*

However, before you start selecting keywords, you will first need to decide on your bidding price. Next to **Bid** is a bar that reads **Suggested bid**. Clicking on this brings up a drop-down menu with the following choices:

- **Suggested bid:** Uses past bidding activity to predict bids that are more likely to win
- **Custom bid:** Can customize bids for each keyword
- **Default bid:** Links multiple keywords to the same bid value

When I first started running Amazon ads, the biggest mistake I made was using the *Suggested bids*. Amazon wants your money, and the *Suggested bids* are much higher than they need to be for ads to be effective. Using *Suggested bids* will quickly eat up your advertising budget, as it did mine. Do not use them!

Instead, I recommend selecting *Custom bid*, which allows you to set the same rate for each keyword. And I recommend that you start your ads with a very low bid.

You will notice that the *Suggested bids* that Amazon provides are pretty high. Most are in the 50-cent to $1 range, while some are several dollars. Instead, enter a low *Custom bid* under 30 cents to start. To be competitive against other advertisers, choose an odd number. Most advertisers are selecting even numbers, such as 20 cents. So, selecting 21 cents can give you an advantage as you compete for ad placements.

Once you have seen your bid rate, it is time to select your keywords. Amazon divides its keywords into three types:

- **Broad:** Your keywords will be matched to search terms that match your keywords AND keywords related to the keyword, including synonyms, misspellings, and variations. For instance, entering the keyword *Ebay* as *Broad* could show my ad next to books that were brought up in a search using words such as *eay* (misspelled), *reselling, auctions*, etc.
- **Phrase:** Your keywords will be matched to search terms that include specific keywords in any order. For instance, the keyword *Ebay* could place my ad next to books that were brought up in a search using phrases such as *selling on ebay* or *ebay sales.*
- **Exact:** Your keywords will be matched only to those that match them exactly. For instance, the keyword *Ebay* would only show my ad to users who searched Amazon using Ebay as their only search term.

When you are just starting out, it is acceptable to select all three options. In fact, Amazon will default to all of these being pre-selected. As you progress in using *Amazon Advertising*, you will likely start to notice which of these types works best for you.

Some advertisers only use one of these types, while others use two or all three. You can also allow Amazon to show you all three and then manually pick the ones you want.

Amazon will present you with a long list of keywords. You can click on **Add all** to select all of them, but I recommend you look at the options as many times irrelevant keywords will be included. For instance, once, I was setting up an ad for an Ebay book, and for some reason, the Amazon system pulled "bay" from "Ebay" and added in all kinds of keywords for a San Francisco Bay area spice company. Clearly, those keywords were not going to help me sell Ebay books, so it was important that I manually click on the keywords I did want to use, passing over the ones I did not.

A new feature within the keywords section is that Amazon will show you the percentage of times a particular keyword leads to a sale, including if the keyword does not result in a sale. I know only select the keywords that have a positive percentage of it, resulting in an order. Since you pay every time someone clicks on your ad, you don't want to waste money on ads that generate clicks but not sales.

When you set up your first ad, look at Amazon's list of suggested keywords, and add each manually, I will choose *Broad, Phrase,* and *Exact.* Not all keywords will likely have a suggested bid amount entered, but that is okay if you still want to choose those keywords using your *Custom bid.* Sometimes the Amazon reporting system lags and does not show the suggested bids. If it is a keyword that you think matches your book, go ahead and add it.

Adding keywords from Amazon's list will put the keywords over into the right-hand column of the ad page. You can go back and delete keywords you decide you do not want before you publish your ad. And even after your ad has gone live, you can still make specific keywords inactive by "pausing" them within the ad. And you can also add new keywords.

Back up under *Keyword targeting,* and next to *Suggested* is *Enter list.* This is where you can manually enter keywords by either typing them in or copying them from a file. A program such as Publisher Rocket will provide you with keywords for your genre of books.

Publisher Rocket: *Publisher Rocket* is a subscription-based Amazon KDP research tool that most self-published authors use, including me. *Publisher Rocket* allows you to research keywords and categories, see what other authors earn on their books, and generate keyword lists for your Amazon ads. You can export your keyword lists to an Excel spreadsheet; from there, you simply copy and paste the keywords into your Amazon ad keyword field. Learn more at *publisherrocket.com.*

I typically use a combination of Amazon's suggested keywords, keywords from Publisher Rocket, and my own. You want to start your ad with as many keywords as possible – literally two hundred or more – to find out where Amazon is placing your ad. You can then whittle down the keywords and only focus on those Amazon uses for your ads.

Once you have chosen all your keywords, the next section is **Negative keyword targeting.** This section is optional, but it can be helpful to weed out potential search terms that Amazon might use to target your ad, despite the keyword having nothing to do with your book.

Let's say you have written a historical clean Christian romance. You likely do not want your book shown to people searching for horror novels or erotica. Remember that your title and book cover may make some customers think your book is in a different genre, and if they find your ad and click on it, you will have to pay for that click even if the person does not buy your book. Entering *Negative keywords* helps prevent Amazon from wasting impressions and clicks on customers who are searching for a different book genre.

I have a Word document where I keep lists of negative keywords for each of my books. When I start a new ad campaign, I can simply copy and paste the list into the *Negative keyword targeting* area. I personally choose to add these keywords as both **Negative exact** and **Negative phrase.**

The next section is **Campaign**, which is where you will choose your **Campaign bidding strategy.** Amazon gives you three options:

- **Dynamic bids – down only:** Amazon will lower your bids in real-time when your ad may be *less likely* to convert to a sale.
- **Dynamic bids – up and down:** Amazon will raise your bids (by a maximum of 100%) in real-time when your ad may be *more likely* to convert to a sale and lower your bids when *less likely* to convert to a sale.
- **Fixed bids:** Amazon will use your exact bid and any manual adjustments you set and will not change your bids based on the likelihood of a sale.

Most self-published authors choose *Dynamic bids – down only,* as this is the best way to control costs. Amazon loves to spend ad money, so only allowing them to use the bid price you set or to lower it ensures that they will not push you over your budget.

Another section offers you the option to **Adjust bids by placement**. You can choose to increase your bid by up to 900% to get it to the **Top of search** (first page) or **Top of Product** pages. These options are for experienced ad users. I have personally found that these types of ads cost too much and do not produce the results as my regular bidding strategy. So, for this example, we will leave this section as-is.

The next section is **Settings**, you will first choose your **Campaign name.** You can start by just typing in the name of your book. As you gain experience with ads, you may start running multiple ads for the same book, so down the line, you may need to differentiate each ad with a different name. The system will not let you give two ads the same name. I typically name my ads by the type of targeting I use, such as *Beginner Ebay: Keywords.*

Next, you will choose **Portfolio**, which is simply the "folder" you want your ad to be filed under. You can create *Portfolios* on the main screen of your account. Until you have done that, the system will default to *No Portfolio*. After the ad goes live, you can create a portfolio and select the ad you want to place in it. I have one portfolio called Active Campaigns, where I file all ads currently running. Amazon does not allow you to delete old campaigns even when you have set them as inactive. I put all my inactive campaigns in a portfolio titled *Inactive Campaigns.*

The next area is for the **Start and End dates** you want your ad to run. Unless you run an ad for a specific promotion, you will likely leave the default date, which is the date on which you create the ad. I only choose an *End date* if the ad is for a limited-time offer. Otherwise, I leave it as *No end date.*

The **Marketplace** section will automatically be selected for your advertising country. If you set up your account in America, the United States will already be selected for you. You can also create separate accounts for advertising in Canada and Mexico.

Next, you need to set your **Daily budget.** I recommend starting with $5. If your ad proves successful, you can always increase your ad spending.

And that is it! You can choose to **Save as draft**; but if you are ready for the ad to go live, click on the blue **Launch campaign** button.

You can edit or end your ads at any time, so don't worry if you made a mistake. I will go over how to edit ads a bit further along in this chapter.

Sponsored Brands: In the above example, we choose *Sponsored*

Products as our *Amazon Campaign Type.* There are two other choices, however: *Sponsored Brands* and *Lockscreen Ads.* Because *Lockscreen Ads* are expensive and geared for seasoned authors, we'll instead talk about *Sponsored Brands* as an alternative to *Sponsored Products.*

Sponsored Brands allows you to advertise multiple books together under on pen name. This is commonly done for fiction authors who have several books within a series. However, I occasionally run *Sponsored Brands* ads for my business books as a way to target readers interested in home-based businesses as well as my low-content books around the holidays when customers are shopping for gifts.

Clicking on *Continue* under *Sponsored Brands* will bring up a listing page very similar to the one we used for *Sponsored Products.* Note that at the time of this writing, Amazon was testing a new layout for the listing forms. By the time of publication, they should all hopefully look like the example we used above. However, there may be some differences in where each section of the form is. How you fill out each section remains the same.

Under *Sponsored Brands,* the *Settings* section is now appearing at the top of the page for most users. This is where you enter the *Campaign Name, Portfolio, Start* and *End dates, Marketplace,* and *Budget.*

The differences in this form will be that you first must select the **Author** (the pen name) for the books you want to advertise. All of your pen names will be available from a drop-down menu. For this example, I'm going to advertise the journals, notebooks, planners, and adult coloring books that I have published under my Jean Lee pen name.

After selecting the correct pen name, the next section is **Products.** Here you will select the books you want to appear in the ad. You must choose three or more products. You can also choose the order the first three books

The next section is **Creative.** Here you will see the *Author* name you choose and the *Author profile picture.* You can edit this photo or change it by uploading a new one from your computer.

The next field is **Headline.** You need to type out a short headline of 50 words or less. According to Amazon, *All Sponsored Brands campaigns go through a moderation process. Follow our policies and recommendations to get your campaign up and running quickly.*

These guidelines can help get your headline approved:

- *Check for typos, misspellings, grammar, and punctuation mistakes.*
- *Don't use text in ALL CAPS, RANDOM capitalization, or CaMel CaSe. We recommend using sentence case instead.*
- *Don't use incomplete sentences and fragments.*
- *Don't add price or other pricing messages in any part of the ad.*
- *Language in your headline must match the locale where the content will show.*

The last two sections are *Targeting* and *Negative keyword targeting,* which are the same as they were under *Sponsored Products.* You can then **Save as draft** or click the **Submit for review** button. It can take Amazon up to a day to approve a *Sponsored Products* ads.

Additional Amazon Ad Tips:

Author Names & Books Titles: You cannot use competitor author names or book titles in your listing when you publish a book. However, you can use them in Amazon ads. If your book is similar to *Harry Potter,* for example, then you can include *relevant Harry Potter* keywords in your ad. In fact, you may decide to have one ad dedicated exclusively to Harry Potter keywords.

Why not put every single competitor author and book into one

BEGINNER'S GUIDE TO AMAZON KDP: 2023 EDITION

single ad? The answer is **Impressions.** Amazon can only put your ad in so many places. Where they place your ad is called an *Impression*. You do not pay for *Impressions;* you only pay for *Clicks*. However, if Amazon focuses on only a few of your keywords, it means your others are being wasted.

You can run as many ads as you are willing to pay for, so creating multiple ads with different targets makes sense. It will also help you see which keywords resonate with customers and which targets you are wasting your money on.

Running Multiple Ads: After a book has started selling for me and has generated reviews, I will often increase my advertising of it by running several ads with one target each. For example, with my *101 Items To Sell On Ebay* book, I might run one targeted ad that focuses on the antiques and collectible categories, another on e-commerce, and another on home-based business categories.

Just as you can choose a *Custom bid* with *Keywords*, you can choose a *Custom bid,* or cost-per-click, for *Product targeting*. Again, I suggest starting with a low bid and monitoring the ad to see how it performs. You can always increase or decrease your bids after the ad has been running.

Bidding Strategy: One advantage targeted ads have over keyword ads is that the cost-per-clicks usually cost less. I have difficulty running keyword ads on my non-fiction books where the bids are less than 50 cents per keyword. But with targeted ads, I can sometimes run a successful ad with bids as low as 20 cents.

The cost to run ads on low-content books is tricker as these books are usually lower-priced and don't sell at the rate of fiction or even non-fiction books. If you have a notebook priced at $5.99, you aren't going to want to spend more than 5 cents on a keyword. And it can be hard to find bids that low on Amazon. That's why I rarely run ads on no-content books such

165

as notebooks and blank journals, only on my higher-priced, low-content guided journals and planners. And even then, I choose bid amounts that are much lower than I pay for my non-fiction books.

Analyzing Ad Date: Regardless of your bidding strategy, you will want to wait a while to see if your ad is actually working. It's tempting to only give your ad a day or two to decide if you want to stop running it, especially if the ad is spending money, but you don't see results. But it's important to wait a bit.

Why do you need to wait to see if an ad is actually working? While Amazon will usually start showing your ad within a few hours after you activate it, their reporting tends to lag. The consensus is to let an ad run for at least two weeks before you make any changes, as it takes Amazon that long to give you adequate reporting. And some authors swear that you need to give an ad at least six weeks to judge its performance.

So how do you check on an ad's performance other than by looking at how much money it is spending? Go directly to the ad within your campaign dashboard and click on it to bring up all the statistics.

I typically keep all my active campaigns together in a folder I have titled *Active Campaigns.* Clever, I know! Some advertisers like to keep different product ads in different portfolios, such as a separate portfolio for each of their fiction series. You can play around to find what organizational method works best for you. But if you do not yet have portfolios, simply click on *Portfolios,* which will bring up all your current ads. And from here, you can click on *Create portfolio* and start organizing your campaigns.

Once you have found your list of ads, you can analyze them all together or individually by clicking on each. Amazon provides users with a lot of information about their ads, which can sometimes be overwhelming. When examining all the ads in one portfolio, you can choose five statistics to show up at the very top of the page. I have found that the most useful of these for my fiction books are:

- **Spend:** How much I have spent on all my ads in a given period
- **Sales:** How much money have my books earned from ads. Note that this is your sales number, not your royalties.
- **Orders:** Number of books ordered from my ads
- **Estimated KENP royalties:** How much money I have earned from page reads as a direct result of someone downloading my book from an ad
- **KENP read:** How many pages have been read as a direct result of someone downloading my book from an ad

However, for my non-fiction and no-and-low content books, which are not enrolled in Kindle Select, I do not need the KENP information. For those books, I prefer the following five statistics:

- **Spend**
- **Sales**
- **Orders**
- **Clicks:** The number of times someone clicked on one of my ads.
- **CTR:** The click-through rate, or the ratio of how often shoppers click on the ad when they see it displayed. This number is calculated as clicks divided by impressions.

Several options are available to customize the data shown at the top of the page. However, it is actually in the grid where your campaigns are that you will gain the most insight and be able to edit your individual ads. If you have a portfolio where your ads are, clicking on it will narrow down your view. You can then customize the graph and filter the results by date range, including:

- Today
- Yesterday
- Last seven days
- This week
- Last week
- Last 30 days
- This month
- Last month
- Year to date
- Lifetime

I always check my daily statistics and month-to-date numbers to gauge better how my ads perform. These date ranges are easy to play around with, so look through all of them to find which ones are giving you the best information.

Amazon offers the following column settings, which you can adjust to your preferences:

- **Active:** Whether an ad is enabled and running or disabled; this column is standard and cannot be removed.
- **Campaigns:** Name of the ad campaign. This is also a standard column you cannot remove.
- **Status:** If the ad is in review, pending, or delivering. Another standard column you cannot remove.
- **Type:** Sponsored Product or Sponsored Brand, and if the ad is Automatic or Manual Targeting
- **Start Date:** Date ad started delivering
- **End Date:** Date ad is scheduled to end
- **Budget:** Daily budget per ad
- **Impressions:** How many times Amazon has shown the ad on their website
- **Clicks:** How many times someone has clicked on the ad
- **CTR:** Click-Through-Rate, which is the ratio of how often shoppers click on your product ad when displayed. This is calculated as clicks divided by

impressions.
- **Spend:** The total running charges for a campaign
- **CPC:** Cost-Per-Click, which is the average amount you paid for each click on an ad
- **Orders:** Number of orders shoppers submitted after clicking on your ad
- **Sales:** The total value of products sold to shoppers within the specified ad frame. Remember, this is the total sale value, not the royalties you earn.
- **ACOS:** Advertising cost of sales, which is the percentage of your sales that you spend on advertising.
- **KENP read:** The estimated number of pages read by Kindle Unlimited customers attributed to a specific ad. Remember that your book must be enrolled in KDP Select for you to earn money from page reads.
- **Estimated KENP:** Estimated royalties from pages read from an ad. The current payout is approximately one-cent per every two pages read.

I know there is a lot of data here, but the good news is that you do not necessarily have to pay attention to most of it. In fact, if you do not find specific data fields helpful, you can adjust the settings only to show the columns you are interested in.

I have my grid settings set to show me the following data:

- **Active, Campaigns,** and **Status** (these are standard settings that cannot be removed)
- **Start Date** (note that I don't include the *End Date* as I never enter an ending date; if I want to end an ad, I do so manually)
- **Budget**
- **Impressions**
- **Clicks**
- **CTR**
- **Spend**
- **CPC**

- **Orders**
- **Sales**
- **ACOS**

The main thing I am always watching is my total ad spend versus sales. I want to ensure that I am making more than I am spending. To do this, I need to know what my royalties are. If you earn $3 for every book you sell and sell ten books from one ad, you would need to spend $30 to stay within budget. You are losing money if you earn $30 but spend $40. On the other hand, if you only spend $10 on an ad but earn $30 or $40, your ad is performing very well, and you might want to add to your budget to make even more.

To explain things further, let me give you two examples of how I personally monitor my ads:

Let's say I have an ad for a fiction book that is set up to target keywords. I set my cost-per-click at 21 cents, and the ad is getting a lot of clicks. However, I am not getting sales from those clicks. The clicks cost me 21 cents each, but there are no book sales or KENP page reads to show for it. Now, since this is a fiction book, I would be concerned and would consider turning that ad off if, after two weeks, I had little to no sales to show for it.

However, if this same ad was for one of my non-fiction books, I might leave it running if I suspected that people were buying my other books after they clicked on the ad. So, if I run an ad for my book *101 Items To Sell On Ebay* that is not resulting in sales, but I see that I have a spike in sales for my *Beginner's Guide To Selling On Ebay,* I might surmise that the ad is increasing my other book sales. I could test this theory by disabling the ad for a while to see if my other book sales drop.

Unfortunately, Amazon does not tell you if someone clicked on an ad for one of your books but ended up buying a different book. I am happy regardless; after all, a sale is a sale. But the only way

I can even guess if a particular ad is leading to other sales is to turn the ad off for a couple of weeks and see if my sales drop.

However, let's say that the ad is working well and people are buying the book I am advertising, which I can see because I am earning more royalties than the ad costs. In fact, the ad is working so well that my $5 per day budget is being used up. It is paying off as I am making more in royalties than I am spending, so I can add to my budget, hoping that more ads will increase sales.

Now let's look at another ad type, one where I have *targeted categories*. Let's say I have set up an ad for my Beg*inner's Guide To YouTube* book to target the *Social Media* book category. The Impressions for the ad are very low, meaning Amazon is not showing it to customers. Why? Well, either Amazon does not believe my ad is relevant to the keywords I have chosen, or my bid rate is too low. It is typically the latter, so this is when I would go into the ad and edit it to increase my bidding.

Editing an ad is easy: Simply click on the ad itself, and you will be taken to a new page where you can see the specific data from the ad, including the *Total targets*, which translates to the keywords or categories/products you choose to target.

Let's say that the ad with the low impressions targets just the *Social Media* category. When I click on *Total targets*, Amazon will bring up a new screen showing me all the targets and my current bid, which we will say is 21 cents. If the impressions on the ad are low, that means that my bid is likely too low. In other words, other advertisers are out-bidding me, and Amazon is showing those ads over mine.

I decided to increase my bid to 31 cents per click for this ad. This ensures my bid will beat out anyone bidding 30 cents or less. Or I could go higher, perhaps 41 cents. Either way, I would then leave the ad running for another couple of weeks to gather more data. If the ad starts getting more *Impressions* but still is not getting

Clicks, I might decide to no longer target that particular category. The same would be true if the ad is getting clicks but is not generating sales.

Note that you can easily **bulk edit your bids.** To do this, simply click on one of your ads. A new page will open. Simply click on the box to the left of the ad. An option to **Adjust default bid** will appear. Clicking on this will open a field titled **Set default bid to ($).** You simply type your new bid amount into the field and then click **Save.** The new bid amount will automatically be applied to the ad.

You will also see a column of *Suggested bids*; just as they were when you initially created the ad, these are the amounts Amazon wants you to spend. They are often much higher than you need to spend. When I started running ads, I would just run down the column and click on all the *Suggested bids,* quickly running out of budget within hours.

I've learned never to use Amazon's suggested bids. And I've also learned to set my bids even lower than the lowest number they tell me most bids are starting at.

If Amazon tells me that the suggested bid for a keyword is 66 cents and that most bids are between 34 cents and $1.10, I will go even lower and enter in 20 cents. If I find that an ad isn't getting impressions, I will simply up the bid by a bit at a time until it does.

Sometimes you are sure an ad will work for specific targets, but for whatever reason, it just doesn't. Hopefully, you will find the keywords and categories your ad does perform well under and focus your time and money on those.

After your ad has been running for a couple of weeks, in addition to the *CPC or cost-per-click,* you also want to take note of the following when looking at each keyword/target:

Impressions: As we just discussed, if an ad overall is not getting many *Impressions,* you might want to increase the bids for each keyword/target. However, what if you have keywords/targets that are getting impressions, but some aren't at all? You have two choices here: disable those keywords/targets entirely and forget about them, or disable them BUT create new ads using just those keywords/targets to see if they would work with new targets.

Amazon wants to make money from ads, but they also want to make money from book sales. So, it is in their best interest for your ads to be successful. If you have an ad with keywords that are getting impressions and sales, that's great; and you will want to focus that ad strictly on those keywords that are working by disabling the keywords/targets that are not.

However, that does not mean that the other keywords/targets are not viable. They may just be getting drowned out by the other more successful keywords/targets. So, it may be worth it to take those underperforming keywords and create a separate ad just for those. You can easily do this by disabling those keywords/targets and typing up a list of them so that you can copy and paste them into a new ad.

This tactic has worked for me on several occasions, so much so that, in one case, the keywords/targets that Amazon was not using in the first ad did better in a new ad. As I stated earlier, it is common for ads to start with hundreds of keywords; but while this works for testing keywords, overall, you want your ads to have only a handful of keywords, ideally less than fifteen. So, disabling keywords and potentially creating new ads is part of the process you will find yourself going through when advertising on Amazon.

ACOS: Another essential piece of data that Amazon provides advertisers is **ACOS,** or **Advertising Cost of Sales**. This data is shown to us both on the main page as well as within each individual ad.

When looking at the *ACOS* on the main campaign page, you are looking at the combined data for all your keywords/targets. **You want ads with the lowest ACOS percentage,** showing you are getting the most results from that particular ad. Anything higher than 50% means you are losing money.

However, sometimes ads with a higher *ACOS* are worth leaving on because they may be driving traffic to your other books. As I have already discussed, I have several books about selling on Ebay. Sometimes I will run an ad on a particular book but find that the *ACOS* is higher than 50% on that specific ad. However, if I see an overall increase in my book sales, that tells me that people may find my other books via that ad. If I feel that is the case, I will leave that ad turned on, even if I am losing a little bit of money on it as I am earning more money overall.

Amazon also provides the *ACOS* for each keyword/target within the ad. I often find that some keywords have an extremely low *ACOS*, which means they work well. But other keywords/targets that are over 50% may not be. If that is the case, I may disable those keywords/targets and focus on those with low *ACOS* percentages.

Search Terms: Another valuable piece of data that Amazon provides within individual ads are **Search Terms.** When you click on an individual ad, you will see *Search Terms* listed in a column on the left-hand side of the page. Clicking on *Search Terms* will show you what exact search terms customers have been typing into Amazon, leading them to see your ad and click on it.

For example, one of my Ebay book ads might show me that a customer typed "thrift store reselling" into the search bar. Because I had "thrift" as a keyword, Amazon showed them my ad. If I see that this particular search term led to a sale, I might consider adding it to the ad or creating a new ad with it. If I want to add it to the existing ad, I must check the box next to it, which will bring up an **Add as keyword** icon. Clicking this icon immediately adds the search term to the ad's list of targets.

On the other hand, if I see that customers are using search terms that are not resulting in sales and are wasting my ad dollars, I can click on those and add them to the *Negative keywords* for that ad and my database of *Negative keywords*.

Bottom Line: Amazon ads are one of the trickiest parts of self-publishing books. There is no doubt that these ads work, but perfecting them takes time. Start with one $5 ad and accept that you may lose some money as you figure out which methods work for your books.

A common phrase with some publishers, especially when advising those just starting on Amazon KDP, is to go low and slow with Amazon ads. Set your bids low and let them run slow, giving them a lot of time to see if they get results.

However, once you gain experience running ads, you may do the exact opposite: set your bidding higher to get the data faster. A higher bid strategy will cost you more upfront, enabling you to see which targets and keywords are working much faster than the low-and-slow method.

Every author has lost money on advertising; it's just part of the business. But I hope the tips and tricks I provided you in this chapter will help you avoid the costly mistakes I made when I first started using Amazon Advertising. Start with one ad for one book to test the waters. In time, you'll learn what works and what doesn't for your books.

CHAPTER TWELVE: GOING WIDE

If you have decided to opt into KDP Select for Kindle Unlimited subscribers to download your books and be paid by page reads, then your eBooks must remain exclusive to Amazon. You cannot sell your eBooks on any other websites, even your own.

However, you can sell paperback books on other websites, regardless of your eBook status. *KDP Select* only applies to eBooks, not paperbacks. So, if your books are available in paperback form, you can increase your sales by selling them on sites other than Amazon.

And if your eBooks are NOT in *KDP Select*, you can also sell those on other websites. Selling your books on Amazon AND other websites is termed **going wide**. This simply means that you sell your books across all platforms, not just Amazon. And while Amazon is the largest bookseller in America, there are other places where customers buy books.

The two most prominent platforms for selling your books outside of Amazon are **Draft2Digital** and **IngramSpark**.

Draft2Digital: Currently, *Draft2Digital* is only available for eBooks. However, they are currently testing a paperback book option, which has been in beta for nearly all of the past year. For the purpose of 2022, we will just focus on them as a place to sell your eBooks. *Draft2Digital* distributes eBooks to the following websites:

- Amazon (if you aren't already published there)
- Apple Books
- Barnes & Noble
- Kobo
- Tolino
- OverDrive
- Biblotheca
- Scribd
- Baker & Taylor
- Hoopla
- Vivlio
- Borrow Box

I bet you saw Amazon on that list and were surprised. Some authors choose to sell their books on Amazon through Draft2Digital because the royalty payout is higher. For example, a book priced at $4.99 on Amazon directly will earn you 70% of the royalties. However, on Draft2Digital, you would earn 85%.

So why would you not want to publish your Amazon books through *Draft2Digital*? One word: **Amazon Ads.**

We discussed *Amazon Ads* in the previous chapter, and the bottom line is that to run an *Amazon Ad* on a book, the book must be published through Amazon. If you publish your eBook through *Draft2Digital* for Amazon, you cannot run Amazon ads on it. That alone is why you want to keep your Kindle eBooks published through Amazon, as Amazon ads can be a critical tool in bringing in sales.

However, it IS advantageous to publish your eBook on *Draft2Digital* if it is not enrolled in *KDP Select* to be sold on the other sites that *Draft2Digital* serves. None of my non-fiction eBooks are enrolled in *KDP Select*, so I have uploaded them all to *Draft2Digital*.

If an eBook is already published on Amazon, *Draft2Digital* will automatically catch it and will not publish it to Amazon. And, if your book is enrolled in *KDP Select* and you try to publish it on *Draft2Digital*, they will also catch that and will not publish your book at all.

Do you have to publish your book to all the websites that *Draft2Digital* serves? No. You can select the sites you want your eBook to be on, although there really is no reason not to select them all.

Note that while paperback continues to remain in the beta testing phase, *Draft2Digital* now offers to publish your audiobooks.

Publishing your eBooks on *Draft2Digital* is incredibly easy; much easier, actually, than Amazon's process. To start, you first need to create an account with them at **Draft2Digital.com.** Just as you did with Amazon, you will be required to enter your financial information so that you can be paid. *Draft2Digital* does not withhold taxes from your earnings but will report your earnings to the IRS. Therefore, you will also need to complete a tax interview, where you will need to provide your Social Security number.

Cost: There is no up-front cost to publish your eBooks on Draft2 Digital. They take approximately 10% of the price your set for your book on any sales you make after the individual sites take around 30%. So a publisher's royalties on Draft2Digital on eBooks is around 60%. That's lower than Amazon's 70%, but since Draft2Digital is distributing your book to multiple websites, I personally feel the smaller cut of the profits is worth it.

Payment: *Draft2Digital* pays users once a month and offers four different payout options:

- **Check** (minimum $100 payout)
- **PayPal** (no minimum payout amount)
- **Direct Deposit** (no minimum for U.S. payouts; $10 for international)
- **Payoneer** ($20 minimum payout)

Note that each store partner has different policies for releasing their royalties. Just as with Amazon, *Draft2Digital* will typically pay you 60-days after the end of the month. For example, you would receive your January *Draft2Digital* royalties at the end of March. *Draft2Digital* will send you individual sales reports from each website and your monthly total from all sites combined.

Files & Formatting: You can upload Word documents directly to *Draft2Digital* in either .DOC or .DOCX formats. As discussed earlier in this book, a .DOC file is a basic Word document, while a .DOCX file is saved as a *Web Page Filtered* document.

Draft2Digital will convert your document into an eBook file, allowing you to double-check the formatting and make changes before your book goes live. As with Amazon, you can upload corrected files anytime if needed. If your book is already formatted, you can upload that version, and *Draft2Digital* will not change it.

There is no style guide to follow with *Draft2Digital*, which makes uploading easy. You do not need to include a title page or copyright page, as *Draft2Digital* will create those for you. And you do not even have to include chapter breaks, although *Draft2Digital* does ask that you mark page breaks by differentiating your chapter headings in some way (bold, centered, larger font).

Book Covers: *Draft2Digital* suggests that cover art is in .JPEG format and measures 1600x2400 pixels. However, they also state that "all we really need is a tall rectangle." If you are looking for freelancers to assist you with formatting and covers, *Draft2Digital* offers a "Partners" page where they link companies offering these services.

ISBNs: As with Amazon, *Draft2Digital* offers free ISBNs for eBooks, although it is always better to buy your own ISBNs outright from a site such as Bowker.com.

Customer Service: *Draft2Digital* has fantastic customer support, so if you are having issues with your file converting the way you want, you can use their *Contact Page* to reach out for assistance.

Promotions: *Draft2Digital* also allows you to schedule promotional pricing for your books, including making them free. Note, however, that this will trigger Amazon to price match your book on their site. So, you do not want to run a free promotion on *Draft2Digital* unless you also plan to have it for free on Amazon.

IngramSpark: *IngramSpark* is the largest distributor of self-published paperback and hardcover books, distributing to 40,000 plus retailers and libraries. Unlike Amazon or *Draft2Digital*, however, you must pay to have your books distributed by *IngramSpark.* This cost is one reason many authors hold back from going wide with their paperbacks, so it may be something you wait to do once you make more money.

Note that while *IngramSpark* offers the option to distribute your eBooks, it is almost universally agreed that it is better to distribute your eBooks through *Draft2Digital* as there is no cost to do so. So, for this section, I will focus solely on publishing your paperback books to *IngramSpark*.

There is no cost to set up an account with *IngramSpark*, and they offer many resources on their site regarding self-publishing. You will need a valid email address and payment information to register an account. You will also have to agree to their *Terms of Service.*

To publish a paperback or hardcover book on *IngramSpark*,

you will need to provide an ISBN. As with Amazon and *Draft2Digital*, *IngramSpark* will provide you with unlimited free ISBNs. However, as I have noted previously, it is always better to provide one you purchased through a site such as *Bowker.com*. As I have already mentioned, I buy my ISBNs in bulk from *Bowker*. It is expensive, but it is an investment in my business. And as a business expense, it can be written off come tax time.

Note that you can only upload non-fiction and fiction books to IngramSpark, not no-or-low content books such as journals, planners, and notebooks.

Cost: The big difference between *IngramSpark* and *Amazon/Draft2Digital* is that you must pay to distribute your book through *IngramSpark*. It costs $49 to have *IngramSpark* publish your physical book copies. And that is for EACH book you upload. In addition, there is the cost of an ISBN. And IngramSpark will only print copies of your book when a retailer or library orders it, so there is no guarantee that your investment will pay off.

This cost is what usually turns people off from self-publishing their physical books on *IngramSpark*. And with *Draft2Digital* working on adding paperbacks to their site, which most people suspect will cost much less than *IngramSpark*, publishing there may be something you decide to wait on.

I have seven of my non-fiction books on *IngramSpark*, but these are books I update every year. If *Draft2Digital* ends up offering paperback publication for less than *IngramSpark*, I will start publishing my new releases on *Draft2Digital*. However, I will not wait for that option if I have a new release, as I am unwilling to leave money on the table. I average around $500 in royalties on *IngramSpark* every month, so for me, it has been financially worth it to pay their fees.

However, I have yet to publish paperback versions outside of Amazon for my fiction books because I am willing to wait for the cost to potentially drop with *Draft2Digital.* And since I make most of my fiction income from *Kindle Select* page reads, I am in no hurry to publish my paperbacks outside of Amazon.

Payment: As with Amazon and *Draft2Digital, IngramSpark* pays publishers 60 days after the end of the month. You can choose to have the money deposited into your bank or PayPal accounts.

Files & Formatting: It's universally agreed upon that IngramSpark's uploading process is confusing. Their system of uploading and converting files is much different than Amazon's. They do have a Help Center section with sections to help with your files and title setup, as well as videos you can watch.

I typically make several thousand dollars a year on IngramSpark, but I would be lying if I said I didn't struggle to upload my new books to their site every year. I find it easier to have my files ready to upload than using their conversion software. I've also struggled with the system recognizing my book's ISBN. I usually solve this issue by uploading to IngramSpark only after my book has gone live on Amazon.

Customer Service: While there is a Facebook group for IngramSpark, the best way to get help from IngramSpark is to message them directly on Facebook. I once wanted to unpublish a book and had to message the company on Facebook to get a response.

Returns: The biggest obstacle to selling paperback books through IngramSpark is that most bookstores will not purchase books they cannot return. And most self-published authors cannot afford to accept returns and do not offer returns as an option, meaning bookstores will not purchase their books.

Why not enable your books to be returned? The bottom line is cost. Bookstores can buy books by the case on IngramSpark. If you enable returns, they can return any books that do not sell. The kicker is that you, as the author have to PAY FOR THE RETURNS. Not just the cost of printing the books in the first place but also the shipping both ways. That means you have to cover the cost the store paid to have the books shipped to them AND the cost for shipping the books back. If you accept returns, you can pay for the books to be shipped back to IngramSpark or shipped directly to you.

Let's say an independent bookstore orders a case of your fiction book. However, half of them do not sell. That bookstore owner could then ship the unsold books back to IngramSpark. The cost they originally paid for the returned books, as well as for the shipping charges, will be charged to YOUR account. You can pay to have IngramSpark ship you the unsold books. Some authors do this to take copies of their books to a conference to sell. But you never know what condition the books may be in.

Most self-published authors do NOT enable returns on IngramSpark, meaning most bookstores will not purchase them. Even self-published authors who make millions of dollars have difficulty convincing bookstores to carry their books unless they can guarantee returns.

So how do self-published authors make any money on IngramSpark? The answer is libraries. Libraries can order single copies of your books. Since libraries are lending out books, not selling them, and because they aren't ordering books by the case, they aren't looking to return books.

But can you make money just from library sales? The answer is yes. In my first year on IngramSpark, I earned nearly $3,000 from just library sales. Most of the sales come in December and January when libraries are closing out their end-of-year budgets and getting new ones for the coming year.

The bottom line with IngramSpark is that while it can be a frustrating platform to upload your books to, it can be worth it to get your books into libraries.

LULU.COM: There is another website for the distribution of paperback books outside of Amazon and IngramSpark, and that is Lulu. Lulu allows you to publish your books for print-on-demand sales on their website and order your own printed copies to sell yourself. Lulu is especially popular for no-and-low content books, which IngramSpark will not print. There are even options that Amazon doesn't offer.

On Lulu, you can create:

- Print Books
- Photo Books
- Notebooks
- Calendars
- Comic Books
- Magazines
- Cookbooks
- Yearbooks
- eBooks

You can create both paperback and hardcover books on Lulu. The site boasts that they offer over 3,000 possible formatting, color, and size combinations. And a big draw is that you can create spiral-bound books, which are especially popular for notebooks and planners. You can sell directly on the Lulu.com site, and you can also order cases of your books to sell yourself.

I recommend Lulu for those who are already full-time with no-and-low content books. If you build a successful brand of notebooks, journals, planners, or activity books on Amazon, then it may be worth your time to also publish those books to Lulu for sale on their website.

That being said, just like with IngramSpark, you have to pay for your books to be uploaded to Lulu. And while you can have your books sold on their lulu.com/shop bookstore, the customer base is small.

Lulu offers a lot of options, especially for no-and-low content books. But the cost, along with a smaller customer base, means it's not worth most authors' time to upload books there.

However, if you build up a large brand, it might be a site to consider. Or, if you want to print your products to sell yourself, it's the best option for printing large quantities at a reasonable price.

Bottom Line: Most authors will start their self-publishing journey with Amazon. If their books are NOT in *KDP Select*, they will then publish their eBooks to *Draft2Digital*. If they are already selling a lot of paperback books on Amazon, they will then expand to *IngramSpark*. And if they build a no-and-low content brand, they might look into selling through Lulu.

My advice is to master publishing on Amazon first, then expand to Draft2Digital, leaving IngramSpark for last, and only consider Lulu if you are committed to building a stationery brand.

CHAPTER THIRTEEN: NO & LOW CONTENT BOOKS

Now that you know all about self-publishing fiction and non-fiction eBooks and paperback books, it is time to focus entirely on the other category of books you can sell on Amazon: Print-On-Demand journals, planners, notebooks, and activity books, also referred to as POD or no-and-low-content books.

We've touched on no-and-low content books several times in this book, but this chapter is dedicated entirely to how to research, create, upload, and promote them.

As we have already gone over in this book when you upload a book file to Amazon in your KDP account, the Kindle eBook option is first, and the paperback option is underneath. Most authors publish to Kindle first and then create the paperback version within that listing.

But did you know that you do not HAVE to upload a Kindle version of a book? Did you know that some books are ONLY available in paperback? That is because they have no (blank) to low (very little writing) content pages inside of them. And since

Amazon only prints them when someone orders them, they are referred to as POD or print-on-demand. These are no-and-low content books, and some make a full-time living only selling these products.

Now, Amazon only prints fiction and non-fiction paperback books when someone orders a copy, so technically, all paperback books are considered POD products. But the term is usually reserved for no-and-low content planners, journals, notebooks, and activity books. Just a bit of Amazon jargon to familiarize yourself with!

To simplify things, from here on out, I will refer to no-and-low content books as POD books.

The POD market has exploded on Amazon. Unlike traditional fiction and non-fiction books, these products have little to no actual writing involved. You do not have to develop a story and are not spending months endlessly typing and editing. You simply find ideas for planners, journals, notebooks, and activity books to create and sell.

Just like Amazon requires paperback books to have both an interior (the pages) file and a cover file for fiction and non-fiction books, the same is true for POD books. In fact, you use the same "Paperback" book option to upload these products as you do for traditional books. The difference here is that you do not upload a Kindle version of your book.

There are four types of POD books that people upload to Amazon:

Journals: Journals can be no-content, meaning they simply have blank or lined pages inside, or low-content, meaning they have some text. Guided journals fall under the latter, with question prompts for people to answer. Like planners, journals can be designed in all sizes. 6x9-inch is the most popular, although larger sizes such as 8x10 and 8.5x11 are good options for people who want a larger book with more writing space.

Planners: Planners can range from daily, monthly, yearly, and perpetual (undated); and in various configurations, such as academic year (July to June) or even two-year versions. The interiors for planners include, at the very least, calendar pages, but they can also include pages for contacts, lists, goals, contact ledgers, etc. A planner can be as straightforward or as complex as you make it. And sizes range from ones that are small enough to fit into your pocket to large books that measure 8.5x11-inches. 6x9-inch is the most popular planner size, especially for customers buying gifts for Christmas.

Notebooks: Most notebooks are considered no-content as they do not contain writing on their pages. However, the pages themselves vary from lined and graphed to blank and divided blocks. Just as with planners and journals, notebooks come in various sizes. Sketchbooks also fall under the notebook category.

Activity Books: A booming category of low-content books on Amazon is activity books for both children and adults. Activity books include puzzle books, coloring books, and educational workbooks.

So, what makes self-published planners, journals, notebooks, and activity books sell so well on Amazon? After all, aren't there already big publishing houses producing these products?

The answer is yes; companies such as Hallmark and Mead produce all sorts of stationery products, including activity books. If you've ever stood in line at a grocery store, you've likely seen puzzle books such as word searches and crosswords near the register. However, what the major publishing houses do not offer is a wide variety of niche-themed items.

You may go to an office supply store to check out their planners and find they have an entire aisle devoted to them. And while they have all sorts of sizes and colors, they are all basically the same.

Planners are even sold in craft stores such as Hobby Lobby and

Michaels. There are all kinds of extras you can buy, including stickers. But even planner companies such as Erin Condren and Happy Planner, who produce fun prints and accessories, are still confined to a relatively small number of releases yearly.

And that is where you can stand out with your own POD products on Amazon. Self-publishing, whether fiction, non-fiction, or POD books, is all about targeting under-served niches. The key to making money selling POD products on Amazon is finding niches that no one else is producing products for.

Instead of creating a bunch of basic notebooks in solid colors, you want to make products targeting very specific people. For example:

- A notebook for elementary education college students who also love to drink iced coffee
- A planner for someone on the Keto diet who is also into yoga
- A guided journal for senior citizens who have retired to Florida
- A guided journal for a newly divorced woman who is also an empty nester and loves cats
- A notebook for teens who attend schools where a wolf is a mascot
- A notebook that features small town names for a specific state
- A coloring book that features only pictures of llamas
- A word-puzzle book that caters to people who love to go on cruises to Europe

Most people who are uploading POD products to Amazon are uploading a LOT of products. I am talking hundreds and even thousands of different notebooks, all with the same interiors but different covers. For most POD publishers, the way they make money is by focusing on quantity, not necessarily quality. They have so many products available that they will inevitably have sales and make money.

However, if the thought of creating thousands of notebooks day in and day out is having you cross POD off your list before you even learn more about it, there is another way to make money with these products. Instead of quantity, you want to focus on quality. And you want to hone in on niches that you yourself are interested in.

Perhaps you are a crafter. Brainstorm all the ways that people craft as well as what things many crafters have in common. A quick walk through a craft store will show you all the different ways people craft, from scrapbooking and knitting to stamping and sewing. Think of designing planners, journals, and notebooks for each activity. Consider creating word searches and crossword puzzles that only feature crafting terms.

If you are into sports, brainstorm all the niche sporting events. People immediately think of football and basketball, but what other sports exist that no one really talks about? A look at the list of Olympic sports will give you your answers. Track and field, for instance, has 44 individual events with participants in high school, college, and at the elite level, as well as in the Paralympics and Special Olympics. Sports, both for the participants as well as the parents and coaches, is a huge market. A planner for discus throwers, a journal for kids on the swimming team, a notebook for wrestling coaches, or a gymnastics-themed coloring book are niche markets that likely no one else is targeting.

Animals, pets, food, academics, music, movies, television, leisure, health, fitness, travel...all of these genres, which already have book categories on Amazon, are also topics perfect for creating POD products. You just need to use your imagination and brainstorm ideas.

And searching Amazon for the POD products that already exist will help you see the possibilities. You will want to differentiate the products that the big stationery companies create from those of independent publishers. Here's how:

Go to Amazon and type in "planners," "journals," or "notebooks" into the search bar. For this example, I will use "planners."

A search of "planners" brings up over 9,000 results. However, when you look under "Department," you will see several subcategories. Click on "Books," and a new search page with over 70,000 results pop up. Yikes!

But don't hit the back button. You are where you need to be to research, self-published planners. If you scroll down the page, under "Book Format," click on "Paperback." The search result number is still 70,000, but if you look at the actual products shown, you will note that most are from self-published authors, not the big stationery companies. You can tell as POD paperback books on Amazon all have bounded spines; none are spiral bound. And you will not recognize any of the authors or publishers as they are all independent.

To further narrow down the search, under "Book Language," click on "English." Then under "New Releases," click on "Last 30 days." Unfortunately, the number of products shown is still over 70,000; but now you are only seeing the most recent products that have been uploaded, almost all of them from self-publishers.

From here, you can start narrowing the list down further by subject matter. The idea here is not to find books to copy but to show you all the various products that people are creating. In fact, go back to the search bar and type in something random, such as "goat yoga journal" or "taco Tuesday notebook." Almost every result that comes up is from a self-publisher.

But are these products actually selling? How can you tell? One quick way is to change how the search listings are sorted. In the upper right-hand corner of the search field, click on the "Sort by" icon and choose "Avg. Customer Review." This will sort the items by those with the best reviews. And the books with the best reviews are typically the ones selling the most copies.

However, just because a book does not have a review does not mean it is not selling. I have a lot of print-on-demand products that have no reviews that sell daily. But the longer an item has been on Amazon's website, the more likely it will be to have reviews.

Seeing what categories the book sells in will also indicate sales. If you don't see the book listed in any categories, it means it hasn't sold yet. But if you see two or three categories listed and the book's rank in each, that means it has had at least one sale.

To see how POD products are selling, you will need software such as Publisher Rocket, which we have talked about several times. With *Publisher Rocket*, you can use their *Competition* analyzer to see what books sell by entering various keywords. This will help you find categories to focus on. You can purchase *Publisher Rocket* at PublisherRocket.com.

For example, a basic search for "2022 Planner" will bring up results ranging from those making $3 a month to others earning tens of thousands of dollars a month. You want to focus on these high earners to figure out how you could make something in the same vein, but that is unique. Again, you do not want to copy someone else's work but find the underserved niches that would benefit from more products being offered for sale.

Publishing humorous versions of normally serious planners is one successful tactic. Using *Publisher Rocket*, I can see that one particular "Teacher Misery Planner" is making nearly $30,000 a month. Funny covers are always a good bet, especially during the fourth quarter when people shop for gifts.

When it comes to successfully selling POD products, you need to think creatively to find unique niches that are underserved. If you decide to pursue POD, you will find that the research part is more time-consuming than creating products. Keeping a notebook nearby where you can jot down ideas is a must, as you never know when inspiration will strike.

Again, finding the self-published books can be a bit tricky as they show up right beside the ones that are traditionally published. However, there are a few ways to tell. First, most self-published POD products are only available in paperback, not hardcover or spiral bound. Amazon is beta testing hardcover books, but for now, most people are only able to self-publish in paperback.

Second, the covers for self-published books tend to be simpler than those from traditional publishers and often feature more text than graphics. There are not amazing covers from those who have self-published their POD products, but once you start learning about POD, you can notice those that are self-published just by looking at the covers.

Thirdly, Amazon will take you to their author page if you click on the author's name. If you see that they have several similar books, which are almost identical with just different covers, they are probably self-published. However, it is also important to remember that many people who self-publish on Amazon use multiple pen names. I have shared with you that I use different pen names for non-fiction, fiction, and POD. But most POD publishers have multiple pen names, such as one pen name for their teacher-themed planners and a different pen name for their cat-themed notebooks.

Just as you want to brand yourself for non-fiction and fiction books, the same can be true for POD, especially if you are making products, such as political or religious items, that could turn off potential customers. Amazon does not limit the number of pen names a self-publisher uses, making it easy to keep your pen names consistent within whatever genre your books are about.

I have a separate pen name for my POD products, so they do not appear next to my fiction or non-fiction books. You might assume it would help sales if all my books were under one name, but I believe it would hurt me as customers would be confused why I write Ebay books and sell notebooks with pug dogs on them. As we've discussed in earlier chapters, I also have separate social media accounts for all my pen names.

In 2022, I created an Etsy sticker shop using the same pen name as my Amazon POD products. I did this as I already had a successful POD brand, and I thought that stickers fell into the stationery category of my journals, planners, notebooks, and coloring books. I have a dedicated website for this pen name at jeanleepublishing.com. Here you can click through to my Etsy shop or directly to the categories of books I have created over on Amazon.

Creating POD Products: Just like you must provide both the interior and cover files when uploading paperback non-fiction and fiction books to Amazon, you must do the same for POD products. After all, these are strictly physical books that people will be writing inside of. However, rather than creating planners, journals, notebooks, or activity books in Word, you need more sophisticated programs for creating POD products. And, of course, you also must learn how to create these types of books.

Interiors: To create a POD product, you essentially must create a planner, journal, notebook, or activity book interior that you can then save as a PDF file. If you are already proficient with programs such as Adobe, this might be something you can do on your own. However, there is a much easier alternative, and that is to purchase interiors.

You can purchase interiors for POD products in one of two ways:

- Buy individual pages or sets from designers and put the files together into a book yourself; OR
- Subscribe to a program that provides templates and the software to create and save your books as PDF files that are ready to upload to Amazon.

Several websites sell complete POD packages that include interiors and the ability to put those pages together into a finished book file. The top two sites are BookBolt and Tangent

Template.

BookBolt: Includes research tools, a cover creator, interior designer, drag and drop editor, 1200+ free fonts, more than one million royalty-free images, and puzzles. Plans start at $9.99 per month. *BookBolt* offers dozens of free interiors under their *Interior Wizard* section that anyone can download for free, including:

- Birthday reminders
- Blank pages with page numbers
- Blood pressure log pages
- Body measurements tracker
- Career plan
- College ruled notebook paper
- Comic book pages
- Daily planners
- Diabetes log pages
- Dot graph paper
- Dot line notebook paper
- Dream journal pages
- Finals planning tracker pages
- Fishing logbook pages
- Fitness calendar pages
- Food journal pages
- Graph paper
- Graph, picture, and notebook combination pages
- Gratitude journal pages
- Guest list wedding planner pages
- Guitar tabs pages
- Habit tracker pages
- Handwriting paper
- Hexagon paper
- House sitting pages
- Lined journal
- Mileage log pages
- Monthly planner pages

- Monthly to-do list
- Mood tracker
- Music sheets
- Numbered pages
- Online shopping tracker
- Password tracker pages
- Personal expense tracker pages
- Pet information pages
- And many more

The paid version of *BookBolt* offers dozens of other pages you can download. There is also an add-on option for activity, puzzle, and coloring books.

In addition to the pages themselves that BookBolt offers, you can also choose the following download options:

- No Bleed
- Bleed
- Sizes from 5x8 to 8.5x11
- Page Count

You simply choose the paper you want, enter in the specifics, and then download the file to your system. You can then directly upload that file onto Amazon, create a cover, and put it up for sale.

As an example, let's make a notebook in *BookBolt*. Under their *Interior Generator*, select the *College Ruled* notebook paper. Click on *Bleed*, select *Paperback 8.5x11*, and enter *100* as the page count. Then click on *Download*. The PDF file of your 100-page notebook will now be on your computer.

After downloading your notebook file, *log into your Amazon KDP account* and *click on the yellow + Create button*. On the second page of your listing form under *Manuscript*, you would *click on the yellow Upload paperback manuscript* and select the notebook PDF from your desktop.

BookBolt also offers an *Interior Generator Pro* where you can create a book interior of 240 pages. This is where you can combine multiple different PDF files and arrange them in book form.

For instance, perhaps you are creating a planner. You have PDFs of calendar pages, contact logs, and to-do lists. You can upload the three different PDFs and then move the pages around using the *Interior Generator*. You can then download that file the same way you did the individual pages and upload that file directly to Amazon.

Another feature of *BookBolt* is its *KDP Keyword Finder*. Note that this feature is only available for paid subscribers. Here you enter keywords for your books, and the system will tell you the keywords that you can use in your listing and in Amazon ads. It will also show you the level of competition for that keyword.

For example, I typed "planner" into the system, generating 14 keywords. The keyword "planner" shows it having "high" competition. However, the keyword "planner for" shows it as having "low" competition. I would ensure to include the keyword "planner for" in my title, description, and keywords within my Amazon listing and in my Amazon ads. For instance, I would likely add "planner for woman mom teacher student" into the keyword field within the Amazon listing.

BookBolt also shows you the most frequently used keywords related to the one you entered. For "planner," it showed me the following:

- Planner daily planner
- Planner for
- The happy planner planners
- Budget planner
- Planner
- Planners
- Planner monthly planner

- Planner with meal planner
- Weekly planner

These frequent keywords give you a glimpse into what customers are searching for. In this instance, we see that "budget planner" is included. That means customers on Amazon are searching for and buying budget planners.

Now, budget planners are a very common product on Amazon. But are there niches that you could create targeted budget planners for?

What about a budget planner for single moms? Or single dads? Perhaps a budget planner for a college student? A budget planner for a retiree? There are hundreds of potential niches you can target to make your budget planner stand out from the crowds.

So, is *BookBolt* worth it? I recommend playing around with their free interior pages as it offers you a great way to learn about creating different sizes and styles of interiors. If you like the interface and plan on creating many POD products, then *BookBolt* can be a good investment. They also offer many video tutorials on their website to walk you through the steps of creating books if you are completely new to the process.

To learn more about *BookBolt,* visit bookbolt.io/.

Tangent Templates: *Tangent Templates* offers an easy-to-use software suite that provides over 100 templates that allow you to create a variety of planner, journal, and notebook interiors. There is a one-time charge of $59 to access their software for life.

Their ready-made POD pages include:

- Blank pages with numbers
- College ruled line paper
- Wide ruled line paper
- Graph paper
- Dot grid paper
- Hexagon paper

- Story paper
- Journal paper
- Sheet music
- Guitar tabs
- Handwriting paper
- Sketch paper
- Knitting paper
- Sermon paper
- Comic book paper
- Recipe paper
- Garden paper
- Book review paper
- Wine review paper
- Habit trackers
- Music review paper
- Checklists
- Password ledgers
- Contact ledgers
- Education planner pages
- Mindfulness activity pages
- Paper games
- And many more

My favorite feature that *Tangent Template* offers is its **Dynamic Templates,** which allow you to customize certain pages. The **Prompts** section lets you create products such as guided journals and other pages where you want to enter text. The **Planners** section lets you create yearly, monthly, weekly, and daily calendar pages with your choice of fonts and features.

You can download pages in trim sizes ranging from 5x8 to 8.5x11 and with bleed or no bleed.

The **Interior Designer** tool allows you to create custom pages. I utilize this section a lot for my business planners as I design many of the pages myself.

The **Tangent Builder** tool allows you to completely assemble your books and save them as PDF files that are ready to upload to Amazon.

Other features include their **KDP Helper**, which allows you to figure interior and cover dimensions, and **Listing Helper** to work on your titles and keywords.

There is also a **Category Explorer.** Note that I personally prefer the category search feature in *Publisher Rocket.* However, if you are just starting out and aren't ready to invest in multiple programs, *Tangent's Category Explorer* is fine to use.

For more information on *Tangent Templates,* visit templates.tangent.rocks.

BookBolt versus Tangent Templates: So which is better: *BookBolt* or *Tangent Templates?* Of the two, I have found *Tangent Templates* to be the more user-friendly option for those new to POD. They have an active Facebook group and a YouTube channel where they post a lot of advice and tutorials and answer questions. Plus, their one-time fee versus a monthly subscription cost makes it more affordable overall. However, POD publishers commonly have both programs, although most start with *Tangent Templates.*

I myself use both programs, although I use Tangent far more than BookBolt. However, I learned POD on Tangent, so I am admittedly biased. The advantage of BookBolt is the free options they offer. Even if you don't end up using the free interiors, just playing around with them is a great way to learn the ins and outs of creating no-and-low content products.

Additional Websites for POD Content: You can also purchase interior pages directly from sites such as **Etsy** and **Creative Fabrica**, where designers sell journals, planners, notebooks, and activity book pages, both individually and in ready-to-upload bundles.

These sites offer countless template pages, including the same type of notebook, journal, and planner pages that you can get from *BookBolt* and *Tangent Templates.* I turn to these websites for activity pages, including those for adult coloring books.

Activity Books: Puzzle, coloring, and workbooks all fall under the *Activity Book* category. These books are more complex to produce, but there is a much larger customer base for these books versus notebooks.

Activity books are similar to fiction books in that people who love them continually look for new ones to purchase. Just as romance readers are continually clamoring for new romance novels, people who use activity books are always looking for new ones.

If you know someone who loves crossword puzzle books, you know how quickly they can race through one. My father loved doing crossword puzzle books, and I was constantly buying him new ones.

The same is true for coloring books, both for children and adults. I personally love adult coloring books and buy one after another. It is one of the reasons I started making my own.

While you can create these types of books from scratch, you can buy ready-made pages and even full books from various graphic websites and individual designers. There are also software programs you can purchase to design custom puzzles, including:

BookBolt: In addition to the journal, planner, and notebook pages we discussed earlier, *BookBolt* also offers access to their Puzzle *Creation Software when* you pay for their *Monthly Pro Plan* for $19.99 per month.

Canva: If you pay for **Canva Pro,** you can use their images for your print-on-demand books. They have some puzzle pages and coloring book images for both children and adults.

Creative Fabrica: Creative Fabrica has thousands of puzzle and coloring book pages available. You can pay a monthly subscription for Creative Fabrica or buy each interior individually. Make sure you are purchasing interiors that come with a **print-on-demand license,** which will allow you to create products for sale. This license is different from a **commercial license,** which is for graphics used on websites and in advertising.

Fiverr: There are designers on Fiverr who will create puzzle books for you, both the interiors and covers.

InstantMazeGenerator.com: Create your own custom maze puzzles for both children and adults. Requires a one-time payment of $67.

UpWork: Just as you can hire designers on *Fiverr* to create activity books for you, you can also hire designers on *UpWork.*

WordUnscramble.io: This free website helps you create both word scramble puzzles and anagram puzzle books.

Covers: Earlier in this book, we discussed how to create covers for paperback books. The same instructions apply to creating book covers for journals, planners, notebooks, and activity books. The only difference is POD products tend to come in larger sizes, such as 7x10 or 8.5x11.

And while there is a market for the 6x9-inch paperback books that most fiction and non-fiction books are also printed, I like to make my POD products a bit larger to help them stand out from the other products on Amazon.

In addition to size, the covers for journals, planners, notebooks, and coloring books tend to use vector graphics rather than photos and are more creative than covers for fiction and non-fiction books. Using different fonts, colors, and patterned backgrounds will help your products stand out from the crowd.

Once you start doing your research, you will notice that many POD products on Amazon are 6x9-inches with black covers. These are from designers using the quantity over quality method. I prefer making a few high-quality products for which I can charge a bit more. However, it is up to you to decide which route to go.

My Process: The easiest way to teach you how to create print-on-demand products is to walk you through my process.

For example, let's say I want to create a dog-themed pug planner. First, I would go to *Tangent Templates* and log into my account. I would then look over their planner pages and decide if I want to create any other unique pages to add to my planner. I also might want to add pages for internet passwords and contacts. Fortunately, Tangent already has templates for these pages. I just need to put the pages together.

For a planner, I would first choose the planner page styles (they offer several). For my planner, I want to add a yearly calendar grid, monthly calendar grid, and weekly calendar grid. I would choose each of these separately and then download each file to my desktop. *Tangent* prompts me to do this, making it a quick and easy process. And if I find a mistake, I can correct it and just download a new file.

Next, I would open *Tangent's Builder* feature, which is what will allow me to put these pages together into one book. I can upload the planner calendar pages I saved from my desktop, and I can also add other pages that are on the site, such as passwords and contact ledgers.

Once my book is laid out in the format I want, I simply choose the size I want my planner to be. I really like the 8x10-inch size as it gives people more room to write versus the typical 6x9-inch size. So, I chose 8x10-inches and downloaded the PDF file to my desktop. Again, *Tangent* prompts me to do this by providing a download icon on the page.

After I have downloaded the file for my planner, *Tangent* also provides me with the cover dimensions. This information is on the same page as the interior creator, and *Tangent* prompts me to download both the template and the measurements.

I then open *Canva* and enter the measurements to create a template for my cover. From there, I can insert commercial-use graphics that I have purchased from sites such as *Creative Fabrica.* I can play around with colors and fonts until the cover looks how I want it to.

Using the cover template graphic from *Tangent* allows me to overlay the actual cover layout over my design to see exactly how it will look once uploaded to Amazon. I can move things around if they are uncentered, including ensuring the spine text is in the correct position.

It is common practice to add text to the back cover of fiction and non-fiction books, as this is what potential customers in bookstores will read before deciding whether to purchase your book. However, it is less common to do this for POD products. I do not include text on the back covers of my basic planners, journals, and notebooks, only for my guided journals and activity books.

Once my cover is finished, I save the file to my desktop. I then log into my KDP account and click on the *yellow + Create icon* to upload a new book. You will go through the same process as when you upload a non-fiction or fiction paperback book, so you must enter a title, subtitle, description, and keywords on the first page. On the second page of the upload process, you will upload your interior and cover files just as you did for your non-fiction or fiction books.

You no longer need to enter an ISBN for no-and-low content books. Amazon no longer gives you a free ISBN for these types of books. But you can provide your own if you purchase one from Bowker.

On the final page of your book's setup is where you will enter the price. The POD market is extremely crowded on Amazon, and since you are creating products with much less text than traditional books, you cannot charge as much as you might typically do. It is common to price basic notebooks at $4.99, with more complex planners and journals in the $8.99 to $14.99 range. You will want to base your price on what similar items are selling for. And you want to generate sales for your books to gain in the ranks.

I often price my POD items very low to start but raise their prices if I start getting sales and especially after getting numerous good reviews. I might publish a notebook at $4.99 to start, but if I'm getting sales and the book gets a couple of good reviews, I might push the price to $5.99 or even $6.99.

Printing Costs: As with non-fiction and fiction paperbacks, Amazon will take out the cost to print your POD books from the sale prices, further cutting your margins. Each book's printing cost depends on its trim size and page count. So, for low-priced books, you may end up with only a few cents in royalties after printing and Amazon fees are taken out.

Amazon will show you how much you will earn for each book's sales during the listing setup to help you price your item. It is typical to make only a dollar or two for no-and-low-content books, so I focus on higher-quality journals for which I can charge more.

High-Volume Sellers: As I said earlier, there is no right or wrong way to approach POD products. I have POD products as just one part of my overall publishing business; it is supplemental income for me, not my primary source of royalties. However, some publishers are only producing POD products, so for them, it is important to have as many products available for sale as possible.

For high-volume POD publishers, the trick they use to create hundreds of products a week is to use the same interiors and only change the covers. Remember the pug planner I used earlier as an example? I could use that same interior file for any number of planners. And I could also easily switch out the graphic on the cover to other dog breeds or other animals. I could easily create dozens of different covers in one day by simply changing one graphic. And then, it is just a matter of uploading each variation onto Amazon.

Creating these multiple variations is a great way to start with KDP, as you will learn the creation and upload process faster and faster as you go along. You may find that you enjoy this type of POD model and want to continue to look for other books you can easily create variations of. Or you may decide to focus on fewer uploads that are of higher quality. Again, the choice is yours.

Marketing & Advertising POD Books: The same advice I gave you in chapters ten and eleven about social media, Facebook ads, and Amazon ads applies to POD books, except for one thing, and that is your per-click bid. Since most POD books are priced much lower than fiction and non-fiction paperback books, you typically need to stick to a very low bid amount. I'm talking five cents or less when it comes to keywords, at least to start.

I personally rarely advertise notebooks and blank journals, and I only advertise planners around the holidays. For the coloring books I offer that have reviews, I will occasionally run a low-bid add to those. I advertise my guided journals priced between $11.95 and $14.95 with higher cost-per-click bids as they earn me higher royalties than my notebooks.

POD as a Business: I look at my POD products as their own individual business, one that is separate from my non-fiction and fiction books. Yes, they are all under my one Amazon KDP account, and their royalties are added to my fiction and non-fiction paperback royalties. Still, I publish them under their own pen name and have separate social media accounts for these products. For me, POD is a way to be more creative than I can with my non-fiction books, so it is something I can work on when I need a break from writing.

Today my POD products account for one-fifth to one-fourth of my total monthly royalties. Sales always explode during the fourth quarter as many shoppers purchase journals, planners, notebooks, and activity books as holiday gifts. My notebooks, journals, and coloring books are considered evergreen products, as I don't ever have to update them or release new versions. I do put out new planners every year, but the interiors are all the same, only the covers are different.

POD is a competitive market on Amazon. But with some research and creativity, you can easily begin earning some passive income with no-and-low content books. My only regret with POD is that I did not start creating these products sooner!

CONCLUSION

Having a published book is a dream of many, but one that few achieve through traditional publishing houses. However, self-publishing brings the dream of having your book in print a reality for millions. Not only does self-publishing give you the freedom to write what you want, how you want, and when you want, but you will also keep a much larger percentage of the profits than you would if you signed a book deal.

Making money by self-publishing books requires a lot more than just writing a book, however. From formatting files, creating covers, and managing promotions, self-publishing takes time and effort. But if you are consistent and follow the advice in this book, you will be on your way to making money self-publishing in no time!

There is an active community of self-publishers online, too. From Facebook groups and YouTube channels, many people are making money from fiction, non-fiction, and POD. Search out this online community on the social media sites you are on and take in the advice being shared. The self-publishing landscape is constantly changing, and you must keep up with the latest developments to ensure your books are not left behind.

Write, publish, repeat is a popular mantra in the self-publishing world. The more books you have for sale, the more money you will likely make. And with every book you publish, your writing, cover designs, and the overall process will improve. I began my self-publishing journey in 2013, and I do things completely differently now than I did then. I hope that by sharing the lessons I have learned here in this book, your self-publishing journey will be easier.

Now, get to writing and making money by self-publishing your books with Amazon KDP!

Are you interested in other ways you can make money online? Be sure to visit my **Amazon author page at https:// amzn.to/3wBF0WF** for all of my business books and planners, including:

- **Beginner's Guide To Starting a YouTube Channel: 2023 Edition**
- **Beginner's Guide to Selling On Ebay: 2023 Edition**
- **101 Items To Sell On Ebay**
- **101 MORE Items To Sell On Ebay**
- **2023 Reselling Planner & Accounting Ledger**
- **2023 Ebay Reselling Planner & Accounting Ledger**
- **2023 Postmark Reselling Planner & Accounting Ledger**
- **2023 WhatNot Reselling Planner & Accounting Ledger**
- **2023 Etsy Vintage Reselling Planner & Accounting Ledger**
- **2023 Etsy Sticker Shop Planner & Accounting Ledger**
- **2023 YouTube Channel Planner & Accounting Ledger**
- **2023 Amazon KDP Author Planner & Accounting Ledger**
- **2023 Amazon KDP Low Content Planner & Accounting Ledger**

ABOUT THE AUTHOR

Ann Eckhart is a writer, entrepreneur, and online content creator based in Iowa. She has numerous books available about how to make money online from home. For all of her books, visit her Amazon Author Page at: https://amzn.to/3wBF0WF

You can also follow Ann Eckhart on these social media sites:

FACEBOOK: https://www.facebook.com/anneckhart/

TWITTER: https://twitter.com/ann_eckhart

INSTAGRAM: https://instagram.com/ann_marie_eckhart

MAIN YOUTUBE CHANNEL: https://tinyurl.com/yxvqtwc7

YOUTUBE VLOG CHANNEL: https://tinyurl.com/mvx84bfw

Made in the USA
Columbia, SC
14 October 2022